CW01095607

SNEAKERS THE COMPLETE COLLECTORS' GUIDE

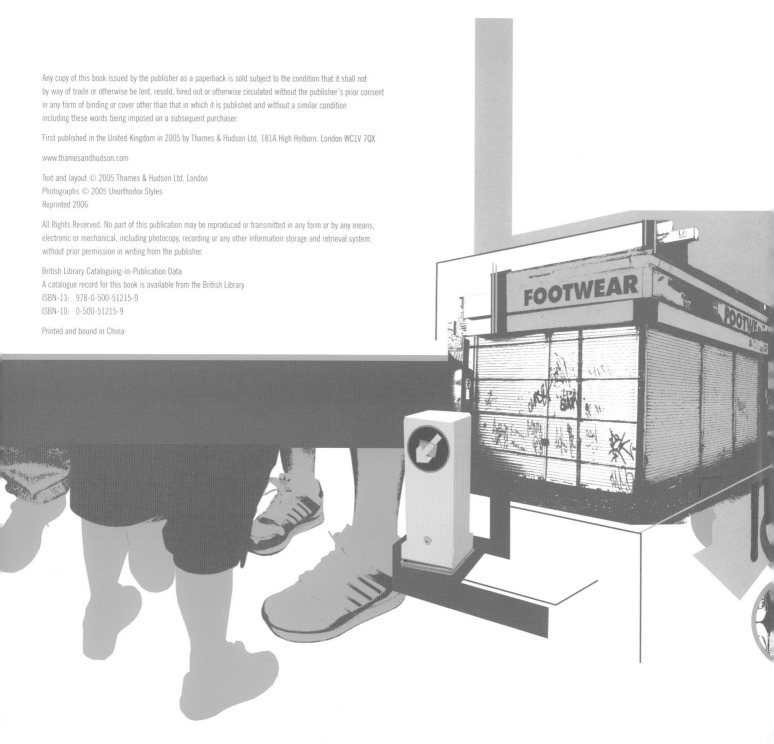

First published in the United Kingdom in 2005 by Thames & Hudson Ltd, 181A High Holborn, London WC1V 7QX

www.thamesandhudson.com

Text and layout © 2005 Thames & Hudson Ltd, London
Photographs © 2005 Unorthodox Styles
Reprinted 2006

British Library Cataloguing-in-Publication Data
A catalogue record for this book is available from the British Library
ISBN-13: 978-0-500-51215-9
ISBN-10: 0-500-51215-9

Printed and bound in China

SNEAKERS THE COMPLETE COLLECTORS' GUIDE

With over 550 colour illustrations

Thames & Hudson

CONTENTS

INTRODUCTION

SNEAKERS, TRAINERS, TURNSCHUHE, BASKETS – WHEREVER YOU ARE IN THE WORLD, WHATEVER YOU CALL THEM AND HOWEVER YOU WEAR THEM, IT IS IMPOSSIBLE TO ESCAPE THE HUMBLE SPORTS SHOE'S RISE TO GLOBAL DOMINATION.

Interest in sports shoe collecting, or rather interest in sneaker culture, has blossomed from being the preserve of hardcore 'sneaker freaks' to a full-blown mainstream phenomenon: you can't walk into a sports shoe store these days without being confronted with a range of fresh designs, old skool favourites, limited edition models and so-called 'rare' shoes, all in a myriad of colourways. Sneakers have moved out from the sports arena and exploded into popular culture as a fashion staple which simultaneously transcends race and class, yet defines who you are in today's urban tribes. This fact has not been missed by the leading brands, which nurture the collectors' market by very carefully releasing or reissuing certain designs or colourways in selected territories, or by collaborating with cult urban fashion labels such as Stüssy or Evisu to produce limited edition shoes that often sell out within hours of their release.

When we started to put this book together, we knew that we had to come from a slightly different angle to that taken by other people on the subject of sneakers. Instead of approaching it from a 'deep in the culture stance', we decided to keep things nice and simple – an encyclopedia of different models, backed up with brand histories and the facts of who, what, where and why. This book is a reference for anyone interested in the world of sneaker culture – from the serious collector with a deadstock collection to die for, to sneaker fans who don't think of themselves as collectors but just happen to own twenty pairs of sneakers (and you know who you are). There are examples and facts to delight and intrigue you all.

Naturally it would be impossible to include every shoe ever released – there are many thousands –

so we have selected over 180 designs which we feel have made a mark on the world. These range from classic designs that have never ceased production, old skool sneakers reissued to a hungry market, shoes with incredible technological innovation, some of the very latest designs, and those which are forgotten masterpieces and deserve recognition today.

Sneaker culture itself stems from many different backgrounds, and – as we will see – certain shoes become indelibly linked with various music genres and subcultures. The relationship to music is one aspect that cannot be ignored. The punk and acid-jazz music scenes, for example, have adopted particular styles as their own. Hip-hop has been one particular genre in which the shoes have been an integral part of the culture. Many rap tracks cite particular models and brands as favourites – and many of those brands offer endorsement packages to key players on the hip-hop scene.

Urban or 'extreme' sports, such as skateboarding, have contributed heavily to the sneaker world as well. These subcultures have developed their own specialized shoes, with an emphasis on the various different technologies that are relevant to their particular activities.

This is not to say that mainstream sports have not played an equally important role: many of the acknowledged classics – from the Converse All Star (pages 70–71) to the adidas Superstar (pages 28–29) – were designed with basketball in mind. The rise in popularity of that game is intertwined with the rise of the sneaker. This game boasts key stars, big personalities, and a huge following of fans, who are sometimes more focused on the shoes than sports. Nike, the new kid on the block compared to stalwarts like Converse and PRO-Keds, has – perhaps more than any other sneaker brand – fully understood the fans' obsession with sneakers, the link between the pro game and urban youth, and, through its publicity and promotion of the top stars, raised the profile of the NBA beyond the US. All around the world there are a whole host of people who have not seen a basketball game but know who Michael Jordan is.

The major brands have always reacted to the trends as they develop, sometimes quicker than others. For example, as a street skateboarding boom took off in the 1980s, adidas released the Superskate (pages 30–31), and as aerobics became *the* fitness craze in the early 1980s, Reebok released the Freestyle (page 209), one of the most successful sneakers of all time. The sneaker collectors' market has developed in a similar way. The brands react to the demand, but are often careful in the timing, location and the number of shoes released. All of this makes the serious sneaker fan's obsession grow, with some shoes developing an almost mythical identity – rumour and hearsay, sometimes deliberately fostered by the brands, is very much part of the sneaker collectors' world.

So where did this all begin? Where did the first sneakers originate? The jury is still out on that one. In terms of oldest brands, you can take your

pick between the Converse, whose Chuck Taylor All Star dates from 1923 (but had been produced without the Chuck Taylor name as early as 1917) and PRO-Keds, which was originally incorporated as Keds in 1917. The technology of using vulcanized rubber to make the soles of shoes had been around since the end of the 19th century – early sneakers were simply a way for the manufacturers to use excess rubber from other production lines at their plants. Those early designs have been lost in the mists of time, and in this book we are concerned only with the brands and designs that are true classics and collectable. From those humble beginnings sprang an industry that has embraced rubber and plastic technology like no other part of footwear design or fashion.

A glance at the technology available on modern sneakers shows a range of plastics and rubber types that would test a chemistry graduate – EVA and TPU (that's Ethylene Vinyl Acetate and Thermoplastic Urethane to those of you taking notes at the front) are used in many sneakers, particularly in the area of motion control, something that is particularly critical for running shoes if wearers are to avoid injury. The notorious wear and tear that a basketball sneaker is subjected to in the pro game has led to many technological and design advances and the use of increasingly exotic materials and methods of production, such as injection moulding. Add to that the plethora of proprietary technology – with such familiar terms as Air, Pump, Disc and Torsion – and you have shoe designs that are a far cry from the simple rubber sole with a canvas upper of the early days.

Sneaker collecting began when companies started to offer more than one model and then more than one colourway of one model – it's as simple as that. Brand loyalty plays a big part, and often loyalty to one

REEBOK PUMP OMNI (see page 223)

NIKE AIR JORDAN I (see pages 148–149)

ADIDAS ZX 700 (see page 54)

design within a brand is a factor too. Early collectors began stocking up on models and colours that they liked and, as the ranges increased, so did fans' collections. It is not uncommon to find people with large collections of shoes simply because they have kept all their old models instead of throwing them out when they buy a new pair. In time, the early collectors have found that those old models are sometimes worth quite a lot of money. Around the world, those early collectors can be seen to be associated with various subcultures. In the US, basketball culture, with its obsession with shoes, celebrity endorsements and the range of team colourways on offer, has been a hotbed of activity since the late 1960s. In the UK, the soccer casual, immaculately turned out on a Saturday in the early 1980s, is a key figure on the sneaker scene, often making journeys to France, Germany and Italy to locate rare adidas and Puma models unavailable at home. In Japan, sneaker culture has been a widespread youth obsession since the late 1980s and has proved to be one of the key markets for the major brands – the insatiable lust of some Japanese fans for a sneaker with a Nike swoosh is legendary. What all of these fans have in common is a love of sneakers, not only because they are 'cool', but because the brands and designs are an indelible part of their identity – you are what you wear.

Not surprisingly, collectors vary tremendously from person to person. What is deemed collectable by one individual may not be appealing to the next person. The price of shoes can vary from $50 for a new pair of Converse All Stars to over $1,000 for limited edition designs or rare originals, such as the adidas Jabbar (page 22). Some collectors have achieved cult celebrity within the sneaker world – people like Bobbito Garcia have become acknowledged authorities on their subject.

In recent years, the array of stores selling sneakers and the sheer number available have changed dramatically. More and more classics have been re-released, and international chain stores have brought a selection to town and city centres around the world as never before.

The Internet plays an ever greater role. Some websites act as online stores or auction houses, with heated bidding among those wanting to buy rare or premium designs, while others provide a wealth of information and have active communities of users who share information with each other. Watching and monitoring these websites has become essential to the brands, as they try to keep these core consumers loyal to their products and identify new trends as they develop.

From humble origins over a hundred years ago, we now have major international brands producing shoes that have become a cornerstone of popular culture, sports and fashion for a growing army of admirers. We think it's time you saw the shoes…

NEW BALANCE 576 (see pages 92–93)

ANATOMY OF A SHOE

SNEAKERS ARE DESIGNED IN ALL DIFFERENT SHAPES AND SIZES. HOWEVER, WHEN IT COMES TO THE CRUNCH, THEY ALL FEATURE THE BASIC PARTS NEEDED TO PRODUCE A GREAT SHOE. ON THESE PAGES IS A GUIDE TO EXPLAIN THE PURPOSE OF THOSE PARTS, AS WELL AS A GLOSSARY OF SOME OF THOSE TRICKY TECHNICAL TERMS.

1. THE TOE BOX

This area is usually perforated if leather has been used. On running shoes, this section is made of nylon. It's a well-ventilated area to minimize heat build-up.

2. MIDSOLE

This is the section between the upper and the outsole. This section of the shoe is where a majority of the shoe technology is applied or encapsulated.

3. OUTSOLE

Hard-wearing rubber is generally used here. Brands design different outsoles for different shoe purposes. Most basketball shoes have a pivot point: a circular pattern found in the forefoot. This part of the shoe is either stitched or bonded to the upper.

4. FOREFOOT

This is the section at the front of the shoe, just under the ball of the foot. Manufacturers design flexible grooves here to ease movement.

5. HEEL

This is at the rear of the shoe. Manufacturers always concentrate on cushioning in this part of the shoe.

6. EYELETS

Eyelets – or eyestays as they are sometimes called – are used for either speed lacing or for added stability.

7. INNERSOLE

The innersole – sometimes called the sockliner – is there to provide extra cushioning. It features a heel cup and arch support. These two features provide stability.

8. TONGUE

The tongue – or on more modern shoes, the 'inner sleeve' – is there to add support and to provide the foot with a custom fit.

9. SHOELACES

These hold the shoe in place.

10. HEEL PATCH AND SIDE PANEL

This is a prime spot that is usually branded by the manufacturer.

11. ANKLE COLLAR OR ANKLE SUPPORT

The ankle collar is reinforced or padded for comfort and support. This is particularly true of high-top basketball shoes.

TECHNICAL GLOSSARY

3M Scotchlite A reflective trim used to enhance visibility at night

a3 technology An adidas rubber-compound cushioning system in the heel or forefoot

ACG (All Condition Gear) A term used by Nike, referring to shoes for outdoor training (sneakers in this range bear the ACG logo)

Air A registered Nike trademark. Pressurized (sometimes adjustable) air pads, used to absorb shock.

APS (Antipronation and Shock Absorption System) An adjustable shock-absorption system used by adidas in the heel area

ClimaCool A registered adidas trademark. A technology that provides 360° breathability and ventilation around the foot.

deadstock A term for vintage shoes that have been kept as new

Dellinger web A web-like material from adidas, which wraps around the midsole to provide stability and shock absorption

Duromesh A breathable mesh material, used on the upper

ENCAP A stability device from New Balance, consisting of an EVA core within a PU shell and designed to disperse shock

EVA (Ethyl Vinyl Acetate) A lightweight material used in the midsole for extra cushioning and shock absorption

Federbein This technology was invented by Puma. It features v-shaped cones of rubber that grip the ground and provide extra cushioning.

Ghilly A D-shaped eyelet used by adidas

Hexalite A cushioning device used by Reebok in the heel and sometimes in the forefoot. This honeycomb-shaped technology is designed to spread shock over a large area.

last A 3D model of a foot, used in the construction process to mould shoes into different sizes and styles

multi-disk An outsole design used by adidas in basketball shoes, designed to improve pivoting, turning and traction

neoprene A synthetic polymer used by Nike on early 90s running shoes, particularly in the Huarache range. This rubber-like material hugs the foot, providing an almost laceless fit.

peg system Used on adidas running shoes, this system allows you to customize cushioning in the heel (in the L. A. Trainer, for instance)

phylite Used in lightweight running shoes in the midsole area, with similarities to EVA

PU (Polyurethane) A synthetic resin, which is not very hard-wearing. Particularly used in the early 80s to create outsoles.

sockliner The innersole of a shoe

soft-cell technology A suspension technology used in the heel of adidas running shoes

S. P. A. technology S. P. A. means 'Sportabsatz' (sports heel). This heel technology was invented by Puma in the early 80s and claims to reduce the risk of injury by 30%.

spoiler flex A device in the ankle collar for extra flexibility

Torsion system Registered adidas trademark. An insert, placed in the midfoot, enhances flexibility, stability and 'torsionability' between the forefoot and rear foot.

TPU (Thermoplastic Urethane) A lightweight and durable plastic stud and outsole material

Waffle Grip Hard rubber waffle studs filled with soft rubber, designed to give extra grip

Zoom Air A Nike technology that uses thin air-filled cushions to enhance the comfort of thin-soled shoes and the forefoot

ADIDAS

The adidas brand shares a common origin with another legendary sports brand, Puma. The Dassler brothers, Adolph and Rudolf, who each went on to found their separate companies, produced their first training shoe in Herzogenaurach, Germany, in 1920. Dassler shoes rapidly gathered a reputation for athletic excellence – Jesse Owens won his four gold medals at the 1936 Olympic Games wearing Dassler shoes – but following a row, the two brothers went their separate ways.

Rudolf went on to found Puma in 1948, while Adolph Dassler started a company called adidas – a combination of his nickname, Adi, and the first three letters of his last name. A lower-case 'a' is always used to distinguish adidas from other brands. A year later, the famous 'three stripes' were established for the company's trademark, which are still used to this day on all its clothing and shoes. The adidas trefoil logo was introduced in 1972, at around the same time as the Munich Olympics. This logo can be found on early shoe models such as the Superstar (pages 28–29) and Stan Smith (page 42), and on clothing such as the A-15 Warm-Up tracksuits and the classic T-shirt.

Adolph Dassler died at the age of seventy-eight in 1972, leaving his wife Käthe to continue running the company. That same year, Dassler became the first non-American admitted into the American Sporting Goods Industry Hall of Fame. Käthe died in 1984, handing over the reins to Horst, Dassler's eldest, who took up the challenge until his death three years later. Keeping the company under the control of the Dassler family – something that is still the case today – enabled its output to be of a consistently high quality and ensured that the brand stayed true to its original guidelines.

One factor that helped adidas to become the dominant force in the world sports market was its sponsorship of legends, such as Muhammad Ali and the German national soccer team – which is quite literally the 'adidas team'. That sponsorship and association with sporting excellence is still the case today – styles such as the popular a3 and ClimaCool ranges (pages 64–65) are worn by top athletes, including soccer players David Beckham and Zinedine Zidane.

Youth culture has always been another contributing factor to the success of the brand. In the 1980s, soccer terraces in the UK were crammed full of three stripes as the soccer 'casuals' developed an obsession with one-upmanship over opposing teams' supporters, with trainers and styles such as the adidas Forest Hills (page 41) and Trimm-Trab (page 36).

In the US, 1980s rap legends Run-DMC – who loved their shoes so much that they composed a song called *My adidas* – wore adidas shoes in their own distinctive style: no laces and with the tongue of the shoe sticking right out. Subsequently, this is a style that has been copied by the fashion world and has been linked back to the hip-hop scene ever since. Run-DMC's shoe of choice (along with many leaders of the growing hip-hop community) was the adidas Superstar, or 'shell toes' as they are often known. The Superstar has become one of the best-selling and most recognizable sneaker models of all time.

Today, the adidas brand effectively consists of three sub-brands: adidas Originals, which is the 'heritage' line; adidas Performance, with cutting–edge contemporary products for athletic excellence; and adidas Y-3, which is a sports / fashion collaboration between adidas and the fashion designer Yohji Yamamoto. Rob Strasser and Peter Moore of Sports Incorporated developed the Equipment concept for adidas (pages 58–59). This footwear and apparel line was introduced in 1991. To tie in with this advancement, a new adidas logo was introduced, which evolved to become the adidas Performance logo featured on most adidas products today.

The continual development of the brand is down to the clever marketing of the key models, the forward-thinking of the adidas team and an awareness of the rich heritage of the brand. Sponsorship of events and the creation of limited products that go beyond simple shoe endorsements have meant that adidas is still one of the most exciting sports brands.

ADIDAS **CENTENNIAL**

THIS FUTURISTIC-LOOKING
MODEL WAS PACKED WITH ALL
THE LATEST TECHNOLOGY.

The adidas Centennial high top was originally made in France and came
in either suede or leather. The suede edition was available in navy, grey,
brown, burgundy or black, while the leather variant was produced in
white / red, white / green, white / natural, and white / burgundy colourways.

The Centennial had several striking features that made it unique –
the distinctive shape of its toe box, for instance, which had never been
used in any other adidas basketball shoe. The multi-disk outsole was
emblazoned with the adidas trefoil to create the maximum branding effect.

The model's overall appearance is quite aggressive. The ridged spoiler flex
on the back of the ankle support, which is reminiscent of tense muscles,
contributes to this effect.

CENTENNIAL

SHOE DATA

FIRST RELEASED
1985
ORIGINAL PURPOSE
Basketball
EXAMPLE SHOWN
Original
NOTES
The Centennial features
the adidas multi-disk
profile sole for added
traction and quick turns.

ADIDAS TOP TEN

ENDORSED BY THE TOP TEN BASKETBALL PROS, JUST AS IT SAID ON THE TONGUE

The adidas Top Ten made an instant impact on basketball courts around the world when it was first released in 1979. The high tops were more extreme than you could imagine, and the padded ankle collar gave the low tops a touch of class.

Over the years, the Top Ten was produced in a multitude of colourways, but the most recognizable is the white / navy, which has a splash of red on the ankle collar. adidas also

created special versions for college basketball teams in exclusive colourways (not available for retail) – for example, a version with a red upper. adidas stopped producing the Top Ten in 1983, but it was reissued in 2002.

ALIFE EDITION

16

TOP TEN

SHOE DATA

FIRST RELEASED
1979
ORIGINAL PURPOSE
Basketball
EXAMPLES SHOWN
Original / Alife
NOTES
In 2003, adidas collaborated with New York artists Alife to produce an all-white Top Ten. ■

ADIDAS ECSTASY

BACK IN THE DAYS WHEN FAT GOLD ROPE CHAINS WERE DEFINITELY IN, THE ECSTASY FITTED IN PERFECTLY.

This high-top basketball shoe was more flamboyant than most, with larger-than-life metallic adidas lettering flowing around the ankle support. It also had a huge trefoil on the side panel instead of the three stripes, and a perforated trefoil pattern on the toe box. These features made it difficult to miss. The Ecstasy was reissued in 2004.

17

ECSTASY

SHOE DATA

FIRST RELEASED
1986
ORIGINAL PURPOSE
Basketball
EXAMPLE SHOWN
Reissue
NOTES
The Ecstasy featured a woolly lining.

SHOE DATA

FIRST RELEASED
1984
ORIGINAL PURPOSE
Basketball
EXAMPLES SHOWN
Originals
NOTES
The Forum was
reintroduced on
to the market in
the mid-1990s.

FORUM

ADIDAS FORUM

THE MIDSOLE FEATURED INNOVATIVE WEBBING.

The adidas Forum was produced in high-, mid- and low-top versions – a first for an adidas basketball shoe at that time. All variants had an ankle strap.

adidas did a lot of experimentation on the upper of the Forum. The use of enamel, for example, was particularly new and refreshing.

In addition, the Forum was sometimes produced in unusual colours, such as chocolate brown, which proved popular with consumers. Surprisingly, however, it was the Forum's $100 price tag that proved its main attraction: it gave the sneaker status.

ADIDAS
REBOUND

IT HAD A SHORT LIFE,
BUT NOW IT ENJOYS
CULT STATUS.

The upper of the French-made Rebound
was a combination of leather and nylon mesh.
These two materials made this basketball shoe
particularly lightweight.

The matching blue ankle support with a touch
of red is rumoured to reflect the colours of the ABA
(American Basketball Association) and is the only
colourway in which the Rebound was produced.

REBOUND

SHOE DATA

FIRST PRODUCED
1980s
ORIGINAL PURPOSE
Basketball
EXAMPLE SHOWN
Original
NOTES
The Rebound was only
produced for one year. ■

ADIDAS METRO ATTITUDE

THIS SHOE HAD PLENTY OF ATTITUDE.

This basketball shoe was manufactured in France and released in a variety of colourways, including white / orange, white / royal blue, and white / blue / orange. The fake lizard-skin editions are by far the rarest: they came in blue / orange, white / black, and purple / yellow. The Metro Attitude was reissued in 2002 in the original colourways.

SHOE DATA

FIRST RELEASED
1986
ORIGINAL PURPOSE
Basketball
EXAMPLE SHOWN
Reissue
NOTES
adidas also produced a modified skateboarding version of the Metro Attitude in 2003.

METRO ATTITUDE

ADIDAS DECADE

WHO SAID THAT HIGH TOPS ARE UGLY?

In 1985, adidas released the Decade. This sleek, high-performance basketball shoe was produced in both high- and low-top versions. The high top featured adidas's patented crisscross one-piece ankle-bracing system, which provided great external and internal ankle support. The wide grip outsole had serrated edges for extra traction and shock absorption. The appearance of the Decade is similar to other adidas basketball

shoes of that period, and the high top resembles the Forum high.

  adidas stopped producing the Decade in 1986, but it wasn't the end of the model. It was reissued in 2003 in brand new colourways, and with a slightly different look. The outsole, for example, no longer features the original multi-disk design. This reissue has meant that the shoe has been embraced by a new generation.

ORIGINAL   REISSUE

21

DECADE

SHOE DATA

FIRST RELEASED
1985
ORIGINAL PURPOSE
Basketball
EXAMPLES SHOWN
Originals / Reissues
NOTES
The Decade was also made in France.

ADIDAS JABBAR

THE FIRST CELEBRITY-ENDORSED BASKETBALL SHOE, BOASTING CLASSIC DESIGN AND TIMELESS SIMPLICITY

Long before kids yearned to be like Michael Jordan, Kareem Abdul-Jabbar's signature adidas model was *the* basketball shoe to have. The memorable advertising campaign for the model included shots in *Sports Illustrated*, featuring a goggle-clad Abdul-Jabbar performing his trademark 'sky-hook' shot. Off court, aside from a brief b-boy association in the early 1980s, the Jabbar has never really been a hot fashion item, but that doesn't mean it comes cheap.

JABBAR

SHOE DATA

FIRST RELEASED
1971
ORIGINAL PURPOSE
Basketball
EXAMPLE SHOWN
Original
NOTES
The original model fetches around $1,000, while later models cost at least $200 per pair. ■

ADIDAS FLEETWOOD

A PREMIUM BASKETBALL SHOE AND A CONTEMPORARY OF THE FORUM

The French-made adidas Fleetwood featured a snake-skin effect on the toe box and the side panel. That wasn't its only distinctive feature: it had a ribbed section on the sides of the ankle support, and the large adidas trefoil on the tongue.

adidas reissued the Fleetwood in 2004. It also brought out a brand new low-top version.

FLEETWOOD

SHOE DATA

FIRST PRODUCED
1980s
ORIGINAL PURPOSE
Basketball
EXAMPLES SHOWN
Reissues
NOTES
The Fleetwood is one of the tallest high-top basketball shoes ever produced by adidas.

24

ADIDAS
AMERICANA

ADIDAS GAVE THIS MODEL
A WHOLE NEW LOOK JUST
BY ADDING SOME COLOUR.

SHOE DATA

FIRST RELEASED
1971
ORIGINAL PURPOSE
Basketball
EXAMPLES SHOWN
Reissues
NOTES
For the reissue of the
Americana in 2003, adidas
offered this model in two
new colourways. ◼

The adidas Americana first appeared in the 1970s on the basketball courts of the ABA. The blue and red adidas stripes matched the ABA's colours.

The Americana has been through some changes over the years. The early models had a mesh upper with a leather toe box, whilst those of the mid-1970s featured a half-suede, half-shell toe box. At the tail end of the 70s, adidas produced a nylon mesh upper with a suede toe box. The Americana was reissued in 2003 in the original ABA colours.

ADIDAS CAMPUS

ONE OF THE GREATEST SNEAKERS OF ALL TIME

This model was originally introduced in the early 1970s as the Tournament, but was renamed in around 1980. Its reputation is such that it is now worn by sneaker fans the world over.

Although associated with the hip-hop scene, the Campus only really gained its cult following after Brooklyn rappers the Beastie Boys started to wear the shoe religiously. The cover of their 1992 album *Check Your Head* immortalized it.

From this launch pad, the Campus was adopted by skateboarders worldwide. Not only did it look good, but it came in a range of great colours and was durable – the construction of the upper rivalled the adidas Gazelle (pages 34–35), but lasted even longer.

The shoe was seen as an excellent lightweight model. Its ability to complement denim was an added advantage.

SHOE DATA

CAMPUS

FIRST PRODUCED
1970s
ORIGINAL PURPOSE
Basketball
EXAMPLES SHOWN
Reissues
NOTES
The shoe received a facelift in the 1990s – the upper was altered, and a Superstar (pages 28–29) outsole was added for increased durability.

ADIDAS
SUPERSTAR

A CELEBRITY FAVOURITE

Introduced in 1969, the Superstar was a low-top version of the Pro Model and was the first low-top leather basketball shoe to be made. Immediately identifiable by its rubber toe box, it became known to millions as the 'shell shoe'.

The styling and chunky fit were soon adopted by key figures on the hip-hop scene, and the shoe reached iconic status when rap group Run-DMC endorsed it. Their track *My adidas* paid homage to the brand and led to the group having their own personalized adidas shoes and clothing.

FRENCH ORIGINAL

REISSUE →

SUPERSTAR

SHOE DATA

FIRST RELEASED
1969
ORIGINAL PURPOSE
Basketball
EXAMPLES SHOWN
Original / Reissue /
A Bathing Ape
NOTES
The original colours were navy, black, red and white, but the shoe has since been produced in different colourways.

↑
A BATHING APE COLLABORATION

Examining the heel and tongue of a shoe can reveal a lot about when and where it was made. The original French-manufactured versions – with the gold and black logo on the tongue – became the most desirable as the shoe's popularity spread to other scenes, such as skateboarding in the early and mid-1990s. The Superstar has since been updated regularly, using an array of elements such as metal eyelets, different types of leather and suede, and rubber that doesn't yellow with age.

Admittedly some reissues do have the gold logo on the tongue, but there are other ways to work out the date of a particular model. A plain sockliner, harder leather and lower stitching on the side of the sole are all signs of a newer version, for example.

To show individuality, customization became a necessity when lacing and colouring these shoes. The adidas Superstar and fat laces go hand in hand.

A BATHING APE COLLABORATION

In 2003, adidas teamed up with Japanese clothing company A Bathing Ape to create a limited edition of the Superstar. Intricate details were added to the basic model. On the white version, for example, the toe was deliberately yellowed slightly to mimic a pair of original Superstars, and other stunning details such as embossing techniques and lace badges made the whole series extremely sought-after.

Four models were manufactured in total: 500 pairs of the three commercially available models, and 100 special all-black limited edition pairs, split between Nigo (the owner of A Bathing Ape) and adidas.

A BATHING APE COLLABORATION

ADIDAS SUPERSKATE

ADIDAS'S RESPONSE TO THE GROWING POPULARITY OF SKATEBOARDING

SUPERSKATE

SHOE DATA

FIRST RELEASED
1989
ORIGINAL PURPOSE
Skateboarding
EXAMPLES SHOWN
Reissue / A Bathing Ape
NOTES
The original Superskate model featured a gum sole.

REISSUE ->

30

A BATHING APE COLLABORATION

The Superskate marked the start of adidas's dedication to building skateboarding shoes. Although its overall design was based on a basketball shoe, the leather toe guard and side panels were made using reinforced, layered leather. This model was reissued in 2004.

A BATHING APE COLLABORATION
In 2002, adidas collaborated with Japanese clothing company A Bathing Ape to produce a special Superskate. Three colourways were produced: white / green, white / black and an outstanding snake-skin effect. Only 500 pairs of each colourway were produced, and every pair came with three different coloured sets of laces and an A Bathing Ape lace jewel.

ADIDAS ADICOLOR H

COMMERCIALLY AHEAD OF ITS TIME, THIS DESIGN GAVE THE WEARER THE OPPORTUNITY TO CUSTOMIZE HIS OR HER OWN FOOTWEAR.

The Adicolor H came with eight different coloured markers, which enabled the wearer to fill in the plain white stripes on the side panel in the colour of his or her choice. The shoe had an attractive basic design, which meant that you still looked good even if your artistic skills weren't up to much!

The popular belief that this shoe kicked off the footwear customization trend is a misconception. In reality, kids had been putting their own mark on their shoes for years by colouring and bleaching basic models. However, adidas did produce the first commercial application of the idea.

SHOE DATA

FIRST RELEASED
1985
ORIGINAL PURPOSE
Basketball
EXAMPLE SHOWN
Original
NOTES
Picking up a pair of originals will never be the same as it was in the 80s. You need working markers to relive the experience.

ADICOLOR H

ADIDAS GAZELLE

DESTINED TO STAND THE TEST OF TIME, THE GAZELLE HAS BEEN PASSED DOWN THROUGH MANY GENERATIONS AND IS STILL GOING STRONG TODAY.

GAZELLE

SHOE DATA

FIRST RELEASED
1968
ORIGINAL PURPOSE
Athletic training
EXAMPLES SHOWN
Reissues
NOTES
A gazelle is a small and slender African or Asian antelope, known for its exceptional speed and grace. ◼

There is much speculation about the Gazelle's original purpose. Its silhouette suggests that it could be an indoor soccer shoe, and over the years it has gained immense popularity with soccer fans, alongside the Trimm-Trab (page 36), München (page 37) and Forest Hills. It has also been suggested that the shoe was designed for running. However, the general consensus seems to be that this model was originally intended as an athletic training shoe.

Whatever its initial function, the Gazelle is certainly a beautiful shoe: the streamlined wedge shape, simple styling and flat sole are topped off with the suede upper to create a classic piece of design. It made a real impact on the early 80s UK hip-hop scene, when the likes of the Superstar and Campus were not yet widely available. It was also good for dancing, as it was really light and came in a variety of bright colours. Today, the Gazelle is still worn by b-boys such as Ken Swift and Flowmaster.

As well as being a huge favourite with b-boys and soccer fans, the Gazelle would not look out of place at indie and acid-jazz venues. It was adopted by Brit-pop groups in the 90s, including the likes of Oasis.

TRIMM-TRAB

SHOE DATA

FIRST RELEASED
1977
ORIGINAL PURPOSE
Training shoe
EXAMPLES SHOWN
Reissues
NOTES
The 1977 version did
not have Ghilly lacing
(D-shaped eyelets). ▪

ADIDAS TRIMM-TRAB

THE INFAMOUS TRIMM-TRAB COULD BE THE ULTIMATE SOCCER-TERRACE CLASSIC.

The Trimm-Trab was released in different
colourways and was made with high-quality
materials: the upper was suede and the sole was
a dual-density PU (polyurethane). This make-up
made it *the* shoe to have in the mid-1980s.

The launch of the Trimm-Trab was followed
by that of the Trimm-Trab 2 in 1984 and the
Trimm-Star in 1985, but it is the original that
remains the most popular. In 2004, it was
reissued by popular demand.

ADIDAS MÜNCHEN

THIS MULTIPURPOSE TRAINING SHOE CAN BE USED FOR A VARIETY OF SPORTS INCLUDING BASKETBALL, HOCKEY, VOLLEYBALL AND BADMINTON.

The adidas München is similar in appearance to the Trimm-Trab. They both have the same PU outsole, but the München's upper is made of nylon mesh with a velour trim, and it has a perforated toe box. The velour trim around the laces is serrated to match the adidas stripes on the side panel.

adidas stopped producing the München in 1984–85, and shoe enthusiasts have been searching for the original version ever since. Even if you manage to track down a pair, be sure not to use them – the PU outsole is not very hard-wearing and may well start to crumble or crack.

MÜNCHEN

SHOE DATA

FIRST RELEASED
1979
ORIGINAL PURPOSE
Training shoe
EXAMPLES SHOWN
Reissues
NOTES
adidas produced a
high-top version of
the München in 1981.

SL 72

SHOE DATA

FIRST RELEASED
1972
ORIGINAL PURPOSE
Training shoe
EXAMPLES SHOWN
Reissues
NOTES
The adidas SL 72 was
reissued in 2004. ◼

ADIDAS SL 72 SL STANDS FOR SUPER LIGHT.

This feather-light training shoe was originally
designed for the 1972 Olympics in Munich.
The upper was constructed from breathable nylon
weave, but the shoe's most distinctive features
were a traction tread outsole, a built-in heel
counter and rubber toe-box reinforcements.

ADIDAS SL 76

THE SL 76 WAS A NATURAL PROGRESSION FROM THE SL 72.

The adidas SL 76 was released in 1976, the year of the Montreal Olympics. It was constructed from breathable nylon and velour, and the number of Ghillys differed depending on the country of production.

The SL 76 was often mistaken for the adidas Dragon training shoe, which did look very similar but was produced in different colourways.

The SL 76 made its TV debut in the cult cop show *Starsky and Hutch* and was reissued in 2004 in the colourway worn by detective Dave Starsky.

SL 76

SL 76

SL 76

SHOE DATA

FIRST RELEASED
1976
ORIGINAL PURPOSE
Training shoe
EXAMPLES SHOWN
Reissues
NOTES
The green / yellow colourway is the most popular with sneaker enthusiasts.

ADIDAS SL 80

THE MOST EXTRAORDINARY FEATURES OF THIS SHOE ARE THE TREFOIL OUTSOLE AND DIMPLED TONGUE.

Just like the SL 76, the upper on the SL 80 is made of nylon and velour. The outsole features an ultra-durable sole at the rear and at the ball of the foot, emphasized with a splash of red.

SL 80

SL 80

SHOE DATA

FIRST RELEASED
1980
ORIGINAL PURPOSE
Training shoe
EXAMPLE SHOWN
Reissue
NOTES
The green / yellow colourway is the most sought-after.

ADIDAS JEANS

THE JEANS LOOKED AWESOME WITH A PAIR OF CORDS.

40

JEANS

SHOE DATA

FIRST RELEASED
1979
ORIGINAL PURPOSE
Training / Running
EXAMPLES SHOWN
Originals
NOTES
The adidas Jeans model was reissued in 2003 by popular demand.

The main attraction of the adidas Jeans was its beautiful blue suede upper. Its vibrant shade of denim blue was interrupted by a splash of yellow between the upper and the outsole, and the gold 'Jeans' lettering.

In 1982, adidas changed the look of the model by modifying both the outsole and the upper. The traction tread outsole was replaced by a trefoil profile outsole, and a new red / navy colourway was added to the range. The shoe's appearance was refined further in 1984.

ADIDAS
FOREST HILLS

WEIGHING IN AT JUST 250 GRAMMES

The Forest Hills tennis shoe was produced in
many different styles during the 1970s and
1980s. The first editions had a protective leather
toe cap, which was similar to the half shells on
the adidas Superstar. The version we recognize
today as Forest Hills was adopted by British
soccer fans during the 1980s.

There are many urban myths surrounding who
wore the first Forest Hills, where they were worn,
which version had a yellow sole, and so on.
This has helped to increase the shoe's status,
cultural-historical standing and fan base.
The model was reissued in 2002.

FOREST HILLS

SHOE DATA

FIRST PRODUCED
1970s
ORIGINAL PURPOSE
Tennis
EXAMPLES SHOWN
Reissues / Originals
NOTES
The 2002 reissue of
the model was released
with various different
coloured outsoles.

ADIDAS STAN SMITH

The earliest version of this shoe was produced in 1964 with the cooperation of French tennis player Robert Haillet. Unlike the later models, it had a thick outsole, no adidas trefoil on the heel and Haillet's name applied to the side. It also had three rows of perforated stripes on the side panel, rather than the normal external stripes.

In 1965, American tennis pro Stan Smith came to the attention of adidas. Haillet's name was replaced with Smith's, and subsequent models had his face and signature on the tongue.

Over the years, the Stan Smith has been a constant presence in the adidas catalogue. It has been produced in a wide range of colours, including red, navy, black and beige, and a Velcro edition was released in the mid-1990s. The sneakerhead's favourite is the original Robert Haillet version.

THE FIRST STAN SMITH WAS RELEASED IN 1965, BUT THIS MODEL WAS ORIGINALLY PRODUCED IN 1964 FOR AN ENTIRELY DIFFERENT TENNIS PLAYER.

42

SHOE DATA

FIRST RELEASED
1964
ORIGINAL PURPOSE
Tennis
EXAMPLES SHOWN
Reissues
NOTES
In 2003, a high-top version was introduced on to the market. ■

STAN SMITH

adidas collaborated with the London store Oki-Ni to produce the Rod Laver NPF, available in five special colourways. The trefoil logo version in particular is a great collectors' item.

The first Rod Laver was white and green with mesh side panels and a leather toe piece and tongue. The second model had similar characteristics to the earlier version and was an instant hit. adidas went on to produce the Rod Laver in a small run of colourways.

The model's smooth sides and minimal branding were influential in its reissue in the late 1990s. adidas experimented with different types of leather uppers, including perforated as well as quilted versions.

ADIDAS
ROD LAVER

THIS HIGH-PERFORMANCE TENNIS SHOE WAS A CREDIT TO ITS NAMESAKE.

ROD LAVER

SHOE DATA

FIRST RELEASED
1970
ORIGINAL PURPOSE
Tennis
EXAMPLES SHOWN
Originals
NOTES
The Rod Laver does not have any side stripes.

ADIDAS
LENDL SUPREME

IN 1984, ADIDAS BEGAN PRODUCING
A SIGNATURE RANGE OF CLOTHING AND
FOOTWEAR FOR TENNIS PRO IVAN LENDL.

There were two unforgettable models in the
Lendl range: the Lendl Competition and the
Lendl Supreme. The former had a breathable
nylon upper with leather trim, and looked a bit
like a low-top adidas Concord with a mesh upper.
The latter was a lot chunkier and was made of
soft full-grain leather, with metal eyelets instead
of the Ghilly lacing system.

   Both the Competition and the Supreme
were produced in a variety of colourways.
The Competition was reissued in 2003
in the original colourways.

SHOE DATA

FIRST RELEASED
1984
ORIGINAL PURPOSE
Tennis
EXAMPLE SHOWN
Original
NOTES
adidas also released the
Lendl Comfort, Lendl Pro
and Lendl Competition.

LENDL SUPREME

ADIDAS EDBERG

YOU HAD TO BE QUICK OFF THE MARK TO GET YOUR HANDS ON A PAIR OF EDBERGS.

This signature model was made for Swedish tennis star Stefan Edberg. An extensive range of Edberg clothing and footwear was produced over the years.

The Edberg is one of the models most cherished by collectors. The yellow and green colourway with a touch of gold is particularly stylish.

EDBERG

SHOE DATA

FIRST PRODUCED
1980s
ORIGINAL PURPOSE
Tennis
EXAMPLE SHOWN
Original
NOTES
Edberg wore the adidas Lendl range at the start of his tennis career.

ADIDAS L. A. TRAINER

THIS MODEL WAS DESIGNED FOR THE 1984 OLYMPICS IN LOS ANGELES.

The three coloured pegs in the heel of the L. A. Trainer are not there merely for cosmetic reasons. They play an important role in the performance of the shoe. The peg system, as it is known, consists of three variable-density heel pegs, which are adjusted to customize the shoe's cushioning. The L. A. Trainer comes with a nylon mesh or leather upper and was reissued in the late 1990s.

46

L. A. TRAINER

SHOE DATA

FIRST RELEASED
1984
ORIGINAL PURPOSE
Outdoor running
EXAMPLES SHOWN
Reissues
NOTES
adidas also released the L. A. Competition, which used the so-called peg system. ■

L. A. COMPETITION

ADIDAS **KEGLER SUPER**

A TIMELESS CLASSIC THAT SEEMS TO GROW OLD GRACEFULLY, YEAR AFTER YEAR.

The adidas Kegler Super also uses the peg system. However, the most interesting feature of this shoe is the suede strip that wraps around the toe guard, extending all the way to the bottom of the shoe to cover the midsole and the outsole. It can be difficult to keep clean, but this somehow adds character as the shoe ages.

The Kegler Super was reissued in 2004. adidas produced a limited edition of 100 pairs, each with an ostrich-skin upper and gold-coloured pegs.

KEGLER SUPER

SHOE DATA

FIRST PRODUCED
1980s
ORIGINAL PURPOSE
Training
EXAMPLE SHOWN
Original
NOTES
The Kegler Super had a similar midsole to the L. A. Trainer, although its outsole design was more like that of the Gazelle.

47

ADIDAS STATED THAT THE MARATHON TRAINER WAS AHEAD OF ITS TIME – AND IT WAS RIGHT!

The Marathon Trainer, known as the Marathon Training in some parts of the world, has a more aggressive appearance than the Marathon 80. The concave trefoil outsole and Dellinger web on the midsole give both versions a futuristic look.

This shoe has gone through some changes since its release in the early 1980s. All of the uppers on the earlier models were made of nylon mesh and velour, but in 1985 the design of the upper was slightly altered. The new models had fewer TPU eyelets than the earlier models, and featured the slogan 'Marathon TR' on the adidas stripes and a flex notch on the toe box.

In 1991, the Marathon Trainer II was released, and 1992 saw the first leather editions. adidas reissued the Marathon Trainer in 2000, and in 2002 special high-grade leather editions were produced in earth-tone colours.

ADIDAS MARATHON

MARATHON 80

MARATHON

SHOE DATA

FIRST PRODUCED
1980s
ORIGINAL PURPOSE
Outdoor training
EXAMPLES SHOWN
Marathon 80 / Reissues
NOTES
The Marathon 80 was the Marathon Trainer's predecessor. The latter was first produced in 1981.

ADIDAS HANDBALL SPEZIAL
GERMAN STYLE, GERMAN SPELLING

OKI-NI COLLABORATION

The adidas Handball Spezial was an extremely lightweight shoe for indoor sports. The upper was made of velour, with additional padding, and the outsole had a four-zone sole construction for the quick stops and turns that handball demands. In 1982, adidas produced the Handball Spezial in white / blue, white / red, and white / black colourways.

SHOE DATA

FIRST RELEASED
1979
ORIGINAL PURPOSE
Handball
EXAMPLES SHOWN
Oki-Ni / Reissues
NOTES
This shoe was worn at the World Handball Championship in Germany in the late 70s.

HANDBALL SPEZIAL

ADIDAS INDOOR SUPER

WHEN HAS A SQUASH SHOE EVER LOOKED THIS GOOD?

The adidas Indoor Super squash shoe is made of nylon but features velour reinforcements. It has an eye-catching toe box and stitching, and a moulded dual-density rubber outsole, perfect for indoor sports. The sole also has insert zones to give greater flexibility and grip. It was reissued in 2004.

THE CREAM OF ADIDAS COURT SHOES:

1 BARRINGTON SMASH

2 INDOOR SPORT

3 INDOOR SUPER 2

4 TT SUPER

5 INDOOR

INDOOR SUPER

SHOE DATA

FIRST PRODUCED
1980s
ORIGINAL PURPOSE
Squash
EXAMPLES SHOWN
Reissues
NOTES
adidas produced a leather version of the Indoor Super in 2004.

OREGON

ADIDAS OREGON

A LIGHTWEIGHT RUNNING SHOE FOR PEOPLE OF ALL SHAPES AND SIZES

SHOE DATA

FIRST RELEASED
1982
ORIGINAL PURPOSE
Running
EXAMPLES SHOWN
Reissues
NOTES
adidas produced a Lady
Oregon in 1984.

Early versions of the adidas Oregon have a nylon upper with pig-skin reinforcements, but after 1983 suede was often used as an alternative to pig skin. The midsole wedge has a Dellinger web to absorb and dissipate shock away from the foot during heel strike. The shoe also features the adidas 'space shuttle' profile and the familiar Ghilly lacing system. adidas produced a special camouflage edition of the Oregon in 2002.

ADIDAS OREGON ULTRA TECH

ADIDAS TOOK THE OREGON TO A WHOLE NEW LEVEL WITH THE LAUNCH OF THIS HIGH-TECH MODEL.

The Oregon Ultra Tech has a synthetic suede and nylon mesh upper, and a reflective trim in the heel area for night-time visibility. Its most striking feature, however, is the thickness of the midsole, which gives it extra cushioning. The Dellinger web emphasizes the size of the midsole, while the rocky-shaped outsole boasts adidas soft-cell technology in the heel.

The original Oregon Ultra Tech was produced until 1993. The shoe was reissued in 2004.

OREGON ULTRA TECH

SHOE DATA

FIRST RELEASED
1991
ORIGINAL PURPOSE
Running
EXAMPLES SHOWN
Reissues
NOTES
The Oregon Ultra Tech was reissued in 2004 in fresh new colourways. Leather editions were also produced.

ADIDAS ZX 500

THE ZX 500 WAS A SERIOUS RUNNING SHOE.

Originally designed as a high-mileage trail and running shoe, the adidas ZX 500 has a nylon upper with velour trim, and is available in a wide range of colourways.

With its TPU heel counter (for added stability) and EVA midsole, it is ideal for anyone who has problems with motion control. All parts of the ZX 500 work together in perfect harmony. This model was reissued in 2002.

ZX 500

SHOE DATA

FIRST RELEASED
1986
ORIGINAL PURPOSE
Running
EXAMPLES SHOWN
Reissue / ZX 700
NOTES
A high-quality leather edition was produced in 2004.

ZX 700 –>

ZXZ NYL ->

ZXZ ADV

ADIDAS ZXZ ADV

ADIDAS WENT BACK TO THE FUTURE WITH THIS MODEL.

The design of the adidas ZXZ ADV pays homage to the running shoes of the 1980s. It combines key characteristics of several 80s shoes – the Dellinger web, for example, which is reminiscent of the Oregon, and the outsole design, which bears similarities to the ZX 500.

The ZXZ ADV was produced in an array of colourways and was extremely well-built. This fooled many sneakerheads into thinking that it was originally made in the 1980s.

SHOE DATA

FIRST RELEASED
2002
ORIGINAL PURPOSE
Running
EXAMPLES SHOWN
Originals / ZXZ NYL
NOTES
The name ZXZ was inspired by a crew of ZX shoe fans from Blackburn, northern England. ◼

ADIDAS
ZX 8000 / **ZX 9000**

THESE MODELS REVOLUTIONIZED RUNNING-SHOE TECHNOLOGY.

The adidas ZX 8000 and ZX 9000 were both produced in 1988 and were the first in a series of adidas shoes to use the company's Torsion system, designed specifically to support the midfoot and allow movement. Not only does this system help to improve running technique, but it also reduces the volume of midsole material in the midfoot area, resulting in a lighter shoe. It is visible on the bottom of the outsole and can even be touched.

The ZX 8000 and ZX 9000 were stunning shoes with head-turning colourways. The later ZX models were popular with the London ragga music scene, and were often worn with jeans or trousers pin-rolled up at the ends. Both the ZX 8000 and the ZX 9000 were reissued in 2003.

57

ZX 8000 / ZX 9000

SHOE DATA

FIRST RELEASED
1988
ORIGINAL PURPOSE
Running
EXAMPLES SHOWN
Reissues
NOTES
In 2003, adidas brought out leather versions of the ZX 9000.

ADIDAS EQUIPMENT RACING

THIS MOVER AND SHAKER
WAS FLEXIBLE BUT STRONG.

The adidas Equipment Racing running shoe was released in 1991 as part
of the Equipment range, which was designed specifically to enhance
performance. It features the adidas Performance logo.

   The Equipment Racing boasts the adidas Torsion system in the mid-foot
area for movement and stability. Its cut-out toe box allows the foot to breathe
and makes this model ideal summer footwear.

EQUIPMENT RACING

SHOE DATA

FIRST RELEASED
1991
ORIGINAL PURPOSE
Training / Running
EXAMPLES SHOWN
Originals
NOTES
All of the shoes in
the Equipment range
were produced in the
same colourway: white /
green / black.

ADIDAS APS

FINE-TUNES THE SHOE'S SHOCK ABSORPTION

APS stands for Antipronation and Shock Absorption System, and it is visible through a window in the heel area. This system allows the individual to adjust the shock absorption of the midsole to suit his or her body weight and ground conditions. The cassette incorporated into the outsole contains PU rods suspended from a TPU shaft. Turning the key clockwise draws the rods together, making the midsole harder; turning the key anticlockwise makes the midsole softer.

The set absorption rate can be checked through the visible window in the heel. In order to prevent over-pronation, the green rods on the inside are harder than the yellow ones on the outer edge.

SHOE DATA

FIRST RELEASED
1986
ORIGINAL PURPOSE
Running
EXAMPLES SHOWN
Reissues
NOTES
This model was reissued in 2003. A high-quality leather edition was brought out in 2004.

APS

ADIDAS
MICRO PACER

ADIDAS TECHNOLOGY TOOK
A QUANTUM LEAP WITH THE
DESIGN OF THIS MODEL.

The Micro Pacer was a high-tech running
shoe with numerous special features.
Its appearance was on another level:
the silver colourway, shoelace cover
and microcomputer were all unique.
The original had a sensor in the big-toe area,
which was triggered when the wearer pushed off
the ground with his or her left foot. When the
person stopped running, the Micro Pacer reacted
accordingly. The shoe's computer sensed distance,
average pace and even calorie burn. Back in 1984,
when the Micro Pacer was launched, this technology
was mind-blowing!
adidas stopped manufacturing the Micro Pacer in
1987, but it reissued the model in 2001 in the silver
colourway, and again in white in 2002. Since then
numerous colourways have been released. In 2003,
a special limited edition was released, packed in a wooden box,
but the original silver shoe remains the most sought-after model.

MICRO PACER NLS

61

MICRO PACER

SHOE DATA

FIRST RELEASED
1984
ORIGINAL PURPOSE
Running
EXAMPLES SHOWN
Original / NLS / Limited
Edition
NOTES
The clock on the reissue
did not work and was
only for show.

WOODEN BOX LIMITED EDITION ->

TORSION SPECIAL HIGH

TORSION SPECIAL

SHOE DATA

FIRST RELEASED
1990
ORIGINAL PURPOSE
Outdoor / Running
EXAMPLES SHOWN
Reissues
NOTES
In 2004, adidas released
a high-top version of
the Torsion Special
in a new colourway. ▪

ADIDAS **TORSION SPECIAL**

YOU WON'T APPRECIATE THE SHEER QUALITY OF THIS SHOE UNTIL YOU'RE WEARING A PAIR!

The adidas Torsion Special was designed for outdoor use, and running in particular. It bears certain similarities to the early adidas ZX running shoes.

This model's upper is made of a combination of nylon, leather and Gore-Tex. It also features the adidas Torsion system in the mid-foot area. adidas reissued the Torsion Special in 2003 in the original blue / yellow / purple colour by popular demand.

ADIDAS **TUBULAR**

CAR TYRES WERE THE INSPIRATION FOR THIS SHOE'S TUBULAR TECHNOLOGY.

The adidas Tubular running shoe featured adidas's Tubular technology, which allows the wearer to customize the cushioning in the heel. This is done using the hand-held air-pump provided – a syringe-style needle that can be inserted into the holes in the outsole. The shoe's U-shaped Vibrastop rear outsole can then be inflated or deflated according to the wearer's requirements.

The front and side parts of the Tubular are constructed from breathable mesh with a webbing overlay. The unusual top piece is branded with the Tubular logo.

TUBULAR

SHOE DATA

FIRST RELEASED
1993
ORIGINAL PURPOSE
Running
EXAMPLE SHOWN
Original
NOTES
This will always be
a favourite among
sneakerheads.

CLIMACOOL

SHOE DATA

FIRST RELEASED
2002
ORIGINAL PURPOSE
Running
EXAMPLE SHOWN
Original 2002 FIFA
World Cup Coca-Cola
limited edition
NOTES
adidas produced
ClimaCool tennis,
basketball and
training shoes. ■

ADIDAS **CLIMACOOL**

THIS SHOE DOES MORE THAN LOOK COOL – IT ALSO KEEPS YOUR FEET COOL.

ClimaCool technology was designed to keep feet cool and dry, even in hot weather. This was the first shoe to be engineered to reduce heat build-up: the ClimaCool system ventilates the upper, innersole and outsole. This combination creates a 360° cooling effect around the foot.

The outsole features a mid-foot rib chassis and air opening, which ventilate the feet from below. These vents provide superb airflow.

adidas produced the ClimaCool in a multitude of colourways and created a special Coca-Cola edition for the 2002 FIFA World Cup.

ADIDAS
A3 TWIN STRIKE

THE A3 COMBINES 1980s STYLE WITH 21st-CENTURY TECHNOLOGY.

The adidas a3 Twin Strike features one of adidas's most innovative shoe technologies. The company's a3 technology works with the wearer's natural foot motion, cushioning and guiding the foot and acting as an energy booster. This technology has since been applied to most categories of adidas footwear.

A3 TWIN STRIKE

SHOE DATA

FIRST RELEASED
2003
ORIGINAL PURPOSE
Running
EXAMPLE SHOWN
Original
NOTES
Every a3 is fine-tuned to the specifics of the sports. ▪

ADIDAS ULTRARIDE

THE MOST DYNAMIC RUNNING SHOE IN ADIDAS'S PORTFOLIO

The most striking features of the Ultraride are the pillars in the heel and the forefoot, which have enabled adidas to create an exceptionally durable, foamless midsole. Foam breaks down over time, but this doesn't happen with the Ultraride. The TPU provides more durability, less energy loss and a faster ride.

ULTRARIDE

SHOE DATA

FIRST RELEASED
2004
ORIGINAL PURPOSE
Running
EXAMPLES SHOWN
Reissues / Oki-Ni
NOTES
adidas is the only
brand to have even
come close to producing
a foamless sole. ■

ADIDAS Y-3 BASKETBALL HIGH

THE PERFECT COMBINATION OF SPORTS AND FASHION

The Y-3 Basketball High is part of the adidas Sport Style range, designed by Yohji Yamamoto. This collaboration combines adidas's sports expertise with Yamamoto's strong sense of style to create a superbly crafted product. There is a low-top version of the Y-3.

The Y-3 Basketball High was made with unusual materials such as stingray print, electric-blue leather and open mesh, and adidas also brought out a limited edition in snake-skin-print leather.

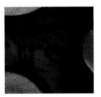

Y-3 BASKETBALL HIGH

SHOE DATA

FIRST RELEASED
2004
ORIGINAL PURPOSE
Lifestyle
EXAMPLES SHOWN
Originals
NOTES
The Y-3 spring / summer 2004 footwear collection was produced to mark the Olympic Games in Athens.

67

CONVERSE

Founded by Marquis M. Converse in 1908, Converse claims to be 'America's original sports company' and it would not be unfair to say that it has become part of the fabric of American popular culture itself. It is best known for the legendary Chuck Taylor All Star (aka 'Chucks', 'Cons' and 'Connies' – see pages 70–71) basketball shoe, which was first introduced in 1917 with the specific aim of enhancing the performance of the wearer and took the name of Chuck Taylor, proponent and player of basketball, in 1923. The Chucks soon became an icon of American sportswear, a position it has maintained ever since. Converse has sold over 750 million pairs of the canvas and rubber classic in 144 countries.

The brand is also renowned for the signature footwear of 1930s badminton champion Jack Purcell (pages 78–79). This model was purchased by Converse from another manufacturer, B. F. Goodrich, in 1972, but is now counted among the company's sneaker classics.

The roots and reputation of the Converse brand lie in basketball, and many basketball shoes in Converse's range evolved from the basis of the original All Star shoe. Both the All Star Pro (pages 74–75) and Leather Pro were worn by such basketball greats as Julius Erving (aka Dr J) and were a prominent feature of the most memorable NBA games from the 1970s and 1980s. The classic One Star (page 73), originally released in 1974, helped Converse to establish a broader fan base and remains hugely popular today – you will see Converse sneakers worn by sports stars and rock stars (Kurt Cobain was a fan), skaters and surfers.

By the end of the 1980s the brand started to struggle, and it hit hard times financially in the late 90s, before being acquired by industry giant Nike. This has put the brand in an interesting position – the oldest American sports shoe brand being bought by the comparatively new kid on the block. The Converse brand had acquired a certain subculture edge to it in the 80s and 90s, so it will be fascinating to see how that audience reacts to the brand being owned by the guys from Oregon.

CONVERSE **ALL STAR**

THIS KING OF THE ALL STARS IS
THE BEST-SELLING SPORTS SHOE
OF ALL TIME.

ALL STAR

SHOE DATA

FIRST RELEASED
1917
ORIGINAL PURPOSE
Basketball
EXAMPLES SHOWN
Reissues / Office editions
NOTES
This shoe featured in
the film *I, Robot*, starring
Will Smith. Its classic
status, history and styling
should ensure that it
continues to sell for
many years to come. ■

The All Star was launched in 1917, but took on the Chuck Taylor name from 1923 onwards in honour of the world-renowned basketball player. Its wide availability and classic styling fuelled its appeal and popularity in those early days, and it has since been adopted by many different sports.

The sneaker's upper is not particularly hard-wearing but is difficult to beat for manoeuvrability and style. During the 1970s and 1980s, the original colours gave way to a raft of different varieties, attracting a whole new consumer base.

At the height of the All Star's popularity, Converse experimented with alternative materials such as leather and denim, and introduced a two-tone fold-down model – a real hit with BMX riders and skateboarders in the late 80s.

Historically, the All Star has also been a favourite in the music world and has been associated with a host of high-profile celebrities and bands, including The Ramones, Fugazi, The Strokes and Snoop Dogg.

CONVERSE **ROADSTAR**

A 1980s TRENDSETTER

ROADSTAR

SHOE DATA

FIRST PRODUCED
1980s
ORIGINAL PURPOSE
Running / Lifestyle
EXAMPLE SHOWN
Original
NOTES
The Roadstar was
reissued in 2002 for
the kids' market. ▰

Although the Roadstar was designed first and
foremost for comfort, it never compromised
its style. The materials used for the sneaker's
upper – nylon and suede – were instrumental
in this respect. A number of colourway variations
were launched.

CONVERSE ONE STAR

THIS STYLISH STAPLE OOZES STAR QUALITY.

It may have always lived in the shadow of the original All Star, but the One Star's popularity in surf and skateboarding circles has helped it to become a symbol of American culture in its own right. The suede edition was particularly sought-after in the 1970s and 80s, as the durability of the sole and flexibility of the upper made it ideal for sports.

Gradually, the One Star managed to attract a professional following. Skateboarder Guy Mariano clearly appreciated the sneaker's qualities and started to wear a pair. Nirvana frontman Kurt Cobain was also known to have favoured the model.

SHOE DATA

FIRST RELEASED
1974
ORIGINAL PURPOSE
Basketball
EXAMPLE SHOWN
Reissue
NOTES
In 2004, Converse produced a special edition for fashion designer John Varvatos.

CONVERSE **ALL STAR PRO**

BIG STARS PLAYED TOP GAMES IN THESE SHOES.

ALL STAR PRO

SHOE DATA

FIRST RELEASED
1979
ORIGINAL PURPOSE
Basketball
EXAMPLES SHOWN
Original / Reissues
NOTES
The All Star Pro was
worn by Julius Erving,
aka Dr J. ▪

The All Star Pro was originally released in the late 70s. Most pairs were white leather, but the high-performance basketball shoe was also brought out in various other colourways.

Later models were more refined: the outsole was thicker and the ankle support more padded. High demand over the years has kept the All Star Pro in Converse's retail catalogue, and it remains a firm favourite among sneaker fans today.

CONVERSE WEAPON

ITS 'CHOOSE YOUR WEAPON' SLOGAN HIT THE TARGET.

The Weapon came in a variety of basketball team colourways, and NBA greats Larry Bird and Magic Johnson both had a pair. This model was brought out in both a high- and low-top edition and featured the Converse Y Bar design. The Y Bar system works by wrapping the shoe around the foot securely, thereby minimizing internal slippage.

  A new version of the Weapon – featuring modifications to the upper and outsole – was introduced in 2004 with an ostrich-skin finish. However, it failed to win over many collectors.

SHOE DATA

FIRST RELEASED
1986
ORIGINAL PURPOSE
Basketball
EXAMPLES SHOWN
Original / Reissue
NOTES
Converse produced a special ostrich-skin edition in 2004. ■

2004 EDITION

CONVERSE **616**

THE HIGH ANKLE SUPPORT ON THIS MODEL PROVIDED THE ULTIMATE PROTECTION.

This early 1990s model was released under the CONS umbrella. It had a large plastic heel strap for extra stability and ankle support, and was specifically designed to appeal to basketball players and fans.

The large white section at the top of the tongue, made from a basketball-style rubber, paid particular homage to the game. The 616 was produced in a handful of colourways.

SHOE DATA

FIRST RELEASED
1991
ORIGINAL PURPOSE
Basketball
EXAMPLE SHOWN
Original
NOTES
Converse produced a mid-cut version of the 616 in 1992.

77

CONVERSE **NBA**

THE LARGE EMBROIDERED LOGO ON THE ANKLE SUPPORT BORE DIFFERENT TEAM COLOURS.

The NBA was a high-performance basketball shoe. It featured the NBA logo on the tongue, and each shoe showed off the team colours. This model's thick ankle support and traction outsole contribute to its somewhat gimmicky appearance.

SHOE DATA

FIRST PRODUCED
1980s
ORIGINAL PURPOSE
Basketball
EXAMPLE SHOWN
Original
NOTES
The Converse NBA was an official NBA-licensed product.

SHOE DATA

FIRST RELEASED
1935
ORIGINAL PURPOSE
Badminton
EXAMPLES SHOWN
Reissues / John Varvatos
NOTES
In 2004, Converse
collaborated with designer
John Varvatos to produce
a special edition model. ▄

JACK PURCELL

THE JOHN VARVATOS EDITION

CONVERSE
JACK PURCELL

AT THE TOP OF ITS GAME

The Jack Purcell, named after the renowned
1930s badminton champion, was originally
produced by B. F. Goodrich, now known as
Goodrich. In 1972, Converse purchased the
company's rubber division and put its own
stamp on the model by adding Jack Purcell's
name. It has since achieved legendary status.
  This sneaker boasts an encapsulated toe
piece, which adds durability and grip to an
otherwise simple upper. It has remained virtually
unchanged since the 1930s, although Converse
gave it a makeover by adding a lightly padded
tongue, a thicker innersole and metal eyelets
to give the shoe a modern edge.

CONVERSE JIMMY CONNORS

JIMMY CONNORS'S DETERMINED PLAYING STYLE WON HIM THE UNDYING LOYALTY OF TENNIS FANS THROUGHOUT THE WORLD.

This Converse shoe, produced in the mid-1980s, was the signature model for American tennis pro Jimmy Connors. The simplistic design didn't reflect Connors's charismatic style of tennis. The Converse star logo was absent from the side panel, but Connors did get his name on the tongue.

SHOE DATA

FIRST PRODUCED
1980s
ORIGINAL PURPOSE
Tennis
EXAMPLE SHOWN
Original
NOTES
Jimmy Connors played his best tennis without wearing his Converse. He sported Converse socks, but played his matches in a pair of Nike Air Tech Challenge. ■

JIMMY CONNORS

CONVERSE **CHRIS EVERT**

EVERT WAS SPONSORED BY CONVERSE THROUGHOUT HER CAREER.

The upper on this particular model was made of smooth leather, and the toe box had small perforations. Tennis shoes in the 80s tended to be simple and understated in accordance with championship regulations, and the Chris Evert was no exception.

This shoe was so refined that it didn't need any vibrant colours. The only splashes of colour were grey and silver.

81

CHRIS EVERT

SHOE DATA

FIRST PRODUCED
1980s
ORIGINAL PURPOSE
Tennis
EXAMPLE SHOWN
Original
NOTES
Evert played in thirty-four Grand Slam finals, winning eighteen of them. She won Wimbledon three times, the French Open seven times, the Australian Open twice and the US Open six times.

FILA

Fila's mission – 'luxury in sports' – is a far cry from its humble beginnings. The company was founded in Biella in 1911 and, although its Italian traditions have been key to its evolvement, Fila is now a subsidiary of large US-based conglomerate Sports Brands International (SBI).

Starting off in the textile industry, Fila decided to consolidate its expertise in this field by moving into the sports world in 1973. The company's most important innovation was the development of a tubular cotton rib material for tennis wear. This was followed by the introduction of coloured tennis clothing – the first non-white lines developed for the game.

Swedish tennis star Bjorn Borg has been one of the most famous names to endorse the Fila brand. During his eleven-year career, Borg won five consecutive Wimbledon titles and six French Opens, and led Sweden to its Davis Cup victory over Czechoslovakia in 1975. Borg's popularity was crucial in cementing the long-term success of the cotton rib. Other tennis stars to have worn the Fila logo with pride include Boris Becker, Monica Seles and Jennifer Capriati.

Fila continued to be a major brand in tennis throughout the 1980s and 1990s, but has also made a name for itself in track and field, motorsports, baseball, basketball and soccer. It can also boast the development of a number of technologically advanced materials – such as the Speed Tech, which claims to offer lightness, rapid response and protection for sprinters, and the 3action damping system.

The company branched out into retail in 2001 with the launch of the first 'Fila Sport.Life Store' in Milan, followed by similar outlets in Paris and Tokyo. The brand is now available in a staggering fifty countries worldwide.

84

FILA FITNESS / F13

THIS MODEL SEEMED TO TAKE OVER...
IT WAS EVERYWHERE!

Reebok's men's fitness and women's aerobics range hit the market at around the same time as the Fila Fitness. Fila brought out a mid-cut (with an ankle strap) and a low-cut model of the sneaker, which was available in a variety of colourways.

There were two distinct types of colour choice: either one colour from top to bottom, or the outsole and the upper in two different colours. Overall, the most prized colourway was the red upper with navy outsole, but the orange model was the one to have in Europe.

In 2003, the Fitness was reissued as the F13. It boasted a slightly different look: 'Fila' was printed on the rear of the outsole, and the midsole had a three-way colour scheme.

SHOE DATA

FIRST RELEASED
1988
ORIGINAL PURPOSE
Fitness
EXAMPLE SHOWN
Original
NOTES
The reissues are called the F13. ▣

FITNESS / F13

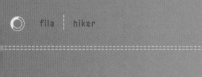

HIKER

FILA HIKER

A SIMPLY STYLED SHOE THAT MADE
A BIG IMPRESSION

SHOE DATA

FIRST RELEASED
1990
ORIGINAL PURPOSE
Outdoor running
EXAMPLES SHOWN
Originals
NOTES
The Fila Hiker had
a similar outsole
to the Trailblazer. ■

Fila brought out the Hiker in the winter of 1990, at a time when outdoor running shoes were in high demand. It hoped to corner the market with the new model and another Fila shoe, the Trailblazer, both of which were available worldwide. But it was the former, with its simplistic design and striking colourways, that won consumers over.

Fila used leather or suede on the upper, and metal D-shaped eyelets and hooks for the lacing system. The brand name appeared on the sole of the shoe four times in chunky lettering, which was great if you wanted to leave an impression in mud or snow.

NEW BALANCE

Massachusetts-based New Balance Arch Company was founded in 1906 by English-born businessman William J. Riley. Initially it offered orthopaedic products, specializing in arch supports and prescription footwear.

In 1934, Riley joined forces with company salesman Arthur Hall. Hall had carved a niche for himself in the shoe market by selling the supports to people with physically demanding jobs, such as policemen.

By the 1950s, however, the benefits of New Balance products had made such an impression that athletes were approaching the company for bespoke shoes. The management also underwent a reshuffle in 1954 when Hall sold the business to his daughter and her husband Paul Kidd.

The volume of athletic products being manufactured by New Balance increased rapidly – to such an extent that this soon became the company's principal specialism. In 1961, the company launched the Trackster, which claimed to be the first performance running shoe with a ripple sole. It was also available in various widths.

New Balance again changed hands in 1972 when the Kidds sold the company to entrepreneur Jim S. Davis. By 1976, the company – though still small – had made its name globally, and the breakthrough 320 model won first place at the *Runner's World* magazine awards.

New Balance has since gone from strength to strength and is still regarded as one of the world's most elite sports footwear manufacturers. It now caters for a whole range of different sports, including basketball, tennis and hiking. The 576 model (pages 92–93), initially produced in the 1980s, is one of its most popular sneakers.

NEW BALANCE 030

THE ULTIMATE KIDS' SNEAKER

The 030 was an early 80s running shoe, catering specifically for the kids'
market. Its upper was made of nylon and featured pig-skin trimming.
If only New Balance had produced it in adult sizes!

SHOE DATA

FIRST RELEASED
1982
ORIGINAL PURPOSE
Running
EXAMPLE SHOWN
Original
NOTES
The 030 has yet
to be reissued. ■

NEW BALANCE 574

ITS PRICE AND VARIABLE WIDTH SIZING
WERE REAL WINNERS.

Designed for running, the 574 featured the New Balance ENCAP system in
the midsole for stability and shock reduction. The 574 has proved extremely
popular over the years. The upper is made entirely of leather, or of a suede
and nylon mesh. In 2003, New Balance experimented with new colourway
combinations and styles, using nubuck and nylon mesh, for example.

574

SHOE DATA

FIRST RELEASED
1988
ORIGINAL PURPOSE
Running
EXAMPLE SHOWN
Reissue
NOTES
A cushioning core of
EVA is encapsulated
within a PU shell, which
adds stability and disperses
shock. ■

NEW BALANCE 576

THIS MODEL WAS ORIGINALLY RELEASED UNDER A DIFFERENT NAME.

SHOE DATA

FIRST RELEASED
1988
ORIGINAL PURPOSE
Running
EXAMPLES SHOWN
Reissue / Crooked Tongues
NOTES
At the tail end of the
1990s, New Balance
released the 576 in
nubuck, full-grain leathers
and prototype-only
World Cup '98 team
colours. These are now
highly collectable.

Originally designed for the US market, the 576
failed to meet sales expectations. As a result,
New Balance was left with masses of excess
fabric. A visit to the company's US headquarters
gave the German sales manager an idea: he saw
a window of opportunity for his home market.
The unused material was shipped over to
Germany, and the 576 athletic walking shoe
was born.

Although it was received well and achieved
a good level of sales, the 576 was finally
dropped from production. It returned to the
market in 1997, and soon every sports outlet
in Paris, London and Milan wanted to stock it.

The original pig-skin colours were black,
navy, scarlet feather (red), moulin rouge (orange),
plum wine (purple) and salad green. However, the
576's popularity was attributed to its sleek design
and comfort.

CROOKED TONGUES EDITIONS

NEW BALANCE 577

A SUPPORTIVE SHOE FOR SERIOUS RUNNERS

Back in 1989, when the 577 was first released, the original colourway was navy / grey. This model still forms an important part of the worldwide New Balance running range – particularly in the UK, where it has not been altered in any way and has a loyal, hardcore following.

In 2002, the 577 hit the European market once more when it was reissued in six colourways of high-grade, full-grain leather. The pattern was reintroduced to the Japanese market in a further four colourways: pine / green / white, navy / black Kevlar, brown / shale, and white.

94

577

SHOE DATA

FIRST RELEASED
1989
ORIGINAL PURPOSE
Running
EXAMPLES SHOWN
Reissue / Limited Editions
NOTES
This model was produced for the Israeli army in black / charcoal colourways in the 90s.

NEW BALANCE 580

A SPECIAL COLLABORATIVE MODEL IN LIMITED SUPPLY

In 2003, the 580 was selected for a collaborative project between New Balance, clothing brand Stüssy and Japan-based store Real Mad Hectic. It proved to be an inspired choice: the 580 was already being produced in China and was not particularly well known outside Asia, and the new edition's target markets were Japan and Hong Kong. The untypical colours made this a particularly interesting model, and the embroidery above the heel was distinctive. Its contoured midsole gives the 580 a real edge, and it is available in a variety of leather and suede combinations.

SHOE DATA

FIRST PRODUCED
2000s
ORIGINAL PURPOSE
Running
EXAMPLE SHOWN
Stüssy & Real Mad Hectic edition
NOTES
The high cut to the heel area provides comfort and stability to the foot.

NEW BALANCE 996

THE ORIGINAL GREY / SILVER COLOURWAY WAS CONSIDERED THE BEST.

The 996 became the recommended running shoe for the discerning sportsperson. It was the first New Balance shoe to be made with two different sole lasts (used during the manufacturing process to determine the shape of the upper and outsole): one for narrow width fittings, and the other for the broader foot.

The 996 enjoyed success and had a good reputation, especially in the US. It was the first running shoe to break the $100 price-tag mark.

SHOE DATA

FIRST RELEASED
1987
ORIGINAL PURPOSE
Running
EXAMPLES SHOWN
Reissues
NOTES
This model was reissued in 1998 as a kids' shoe in numerous colourways. Originally it had a cerecom upper, but it was later produced in leather in both lace-up and Velcro styles. ■

NEW BALANCE 1500

WORTH ITS WEIGHT IN GOLD

The 1500's overall shape was narrower and more advanced than the 576 and 577 models. Described by New Balance as the 'closest thing yet to the perfect running shoe', the 1500 broke new ground in the UK by becoming the first sneaker to exceed a £100 price tag. The original colour was grey with blue trim, although the shoe was later reissued.

1500

SHOE DATA

FIRST RELEASED
1993
ORIGINAL PURPOSE
Running
EXAMPLES SHOWN
Original / Reissue
NOTES
The 1500 has been reissued in both the UK and Japan.

NIKE

Nike's seeds were sown in Oregon, the USA, by Phil Knight, a middle-distance runner and accounting student at the University of Oregon, and his coach Bill Bowerman. Their friendship changed not only their relationship to sports, but also the technology of producing sports shoes and apparel, and the way in which sports brands promote themselves.

In 1962, having completed his studies, Knight went on a trip around the world. During his stay in Japan, he took up an ambition he had shared with Bill Bowerman – to start importing Japanese running shoes at affordable prices into the US. Knight contacted Onitsuka Tiger. When he was put on the spot and asked about his company, he bluffed his way through and said that he represented Blue Ribbon Sports (BRS) – the first 200 pairs arrived in the US in December 1963. This was a turning point, and with Knight and Bowerman having invested around $500 each, the company rapidly gained a great reputation with college athletes. Before long, Bowerman was dreaming of ways to improve the design of Onitsuka shoes, and Knight was dreaming of how much more profitable it would be to produce and sell their own shoes.

In 1971, a company employee, Jeff Johnson, thought up the name Nike (apparently while he slept), after the Greek goddess of victory. Caroline Davidson, who met Knight when she was a student attending the same university, was asked to design a logo. She came up with the now world-renowned swoosh – the Nike name and brand were born.

In 1972, following a split from Onitsuka Tiger, the Moon Shoe debuted at the US Olympic Trials. A year later, the middle-distance runner Steve Prefontaine became the first major athlete to wear Nike shoes. In 1974, Bowerman dreamt of a new innovation for the outsole, made by pouring rubber into a waffle iron to create a waffle outsole (go to the Waffle Trainer on page 100 to see how that simple experiment spawned one of the greatest sneaker designs). By 1978, Nike had started to sell its products internationally.

Kenyan marathon runner Henry Reno broke four world records wearing Nike shoes. Tennis ace John McEnroe started to wear Nike products, broadening the brand's visual appeal in the tennis arena. In 1979, the Tailwind shoe became the first running shoe to be launched with a patented air sole. In 1985, Michael Jordan signed with Nike as a rookie, and a whole new line of shoe apparel was created. The Air Jordan (pages 148–149) basketball shoe became one of the world's most popular sneakers.

The Nike Air Max (page 106) was brought out in 1987, along with Nike's first multipurpose shoe, the Air Trainer (pages 152–153). Both catapulted Nike ahead of the competition. The brand has continued to be a leader in sports design and innovation, and has been endorsed by many of the world's most famous sports stars, including Andre Agassi, Ronaldo and Tiger Woods.

Nike's strengths are threefold: an undoubted intuitive sense of what athletes want and need (something that goes all the way back to the track in Oregon), a commitment to technical innovation, and an attitude and outlook towards branding and marketing that has changed the way sports shoes and apparel are promoted forever.

NIKE **WAFFLE TRAINER**

SOMETIMES MISTAKEN FOR THE NIKE CORTEZ...

There were two versions of the Waffle Trainer: the first edition was launched in 1974; the second version, which came out one year later, featured a flared outsole for better stabilization. In 1976, the UCLA colourway was introduced. It was reissued in 2002.

The Waffle Trainer also featured the waffle-iron outsole – the result of an experiment with a waffle iron by Bill Bowerman. This type of outsole was first used on the Moon Shoe.

SHOE DATA

FIRST RELEASED
1974
ORIGINAL PURPOSE
Running
EXAMPLE SHOWN
Original
NOTES
The Lady Waffle Trainer was released in 1977.

WAFFLE TRAINER

100

NIKE MARATHON

SO BEAUTIFUL AND TIMELESS THAT IT SHOULD BE IN A MUSEUM.

The Nike Marathon was made in Japan and was one of the first Nike shoes to have a nylon upper. In the market in general, nylon uppers – a feature of lightweight shoes – tended to be few and far between at that time. The distinctive toe piece, which was made from pig skin, reinforced the upper.

The design characteristics might look simple by modern standards, but the Marathon was considered technologically advanced back in 1972. The heel counter in particular was ahead of its time. This raised area in the heel reduced shock absorption by the foot. Who said that shoe technology only began in the 1980s?

The Nike Marathon represents an important part of Nike's running shoe history and is definitely one to keep hold of!

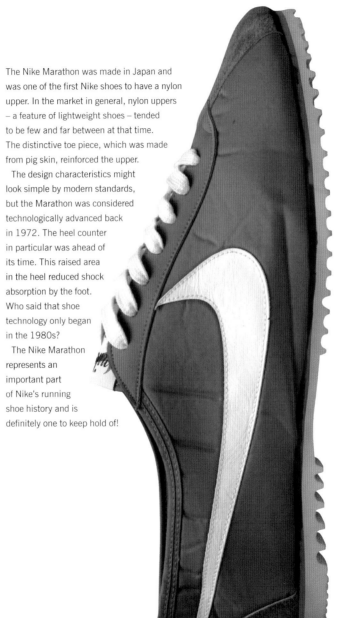

MARATHON

SHOE DATA

FIRST RELEASED
1972
ORIGINAL PURPOSE
Running
EXAMPLE SHOWN
Original
NOTES
It featured the early large belly swoosh, abandoned by Nike in the early 80s.

101

NIKE
AIR SOCK RACER

THE LEMON-DROP YELLOW WAS A BRAVE MOVE.

Nike released the innovative Air Sock Racer in 1985. The one-piece upper design was like no other Nike running shoe before. The breathable woven synthetic mesh upper was reminiscent of a surf shoe, and two straps were used on the top instead of laces.

The Air Sock Racer was worn by Norwegian runner Ingrid Kristiansen, who debuted it at an Olympic trial. The model was reissued in 2004.

SHOE DATA

FIRST RELEASED
1985
ORIGINAL PURPOSE
Running
EXAMPLE SHOWN
Original
NOTES
The original (weak) phylite midsole was replaced by EVA on the 2004 reissue model. ▪

AIR SOCK RACER

NIKE
AIR SAFARI

DESIGNED FOR RUNNING AND TRACK SPORTS, BUT REFERRED TO BY SOME PEOPLE AS A TRAILS SHOE

Considered almost twenty years ahead of its time, the Air Safari wasn't particularly popular to start off with. Two factors influenced this: Nike didn't promote it as strongly as it should have done on its release; and consumers were opting for simpler running shoes with regular colourways. It has since become extremely successful.

The leather upper, which had an unusual style for a running shoe, featured obscure colours such as orange. The speckled grey panels on the Air Safari added further confusion.

The shoe appeared on the reverse of hip-hop artist Biz Markie's album, *Biz Is Goin' Off*. As a result, Biz has become associated with the brand unofficially. The shoe was reissued in 2003 following extra exposure on a sneaker enthusiast's website.

103

AIR SAFARI

SHOE DATA

FIRST RELEASED
1987
ORIGINAL PURPOSE
Running / Track sports
EXAMPLE SHOWN
Original
NOTES
The reissued shoe has enjoyed a fair amount of success, and new colourways have been added. ■

NIKE AIR FLOW

THEY LOOKED LIKE THEY HAD BEEN DESIGNED FOR DUCKS.

AIR FLOW

SHOE DATA

FIRST RELEASED
1989
ORIGINAL PURPOSE
Running
EXAMPLE SHOWN
Original
NOTES
The Air Flow was very much like the Air Current (launched in 1990) – a predecessor to the Air Huarache. Both shoes played important roles in the natural progression to Air Huarache technology. ■

The Nike Air Flow was released as part of the Nike Air International Fall '89 collection, which was marked by bright, versatile colours. It was a lightweight running shoe and boasted an encapsulated heel Air Sole Unit in the midsole for maximum cushioning. The upper was made of nylon, Lycra and synthetic suede, which provided a sock-like fit. This made it ideal for the summer.

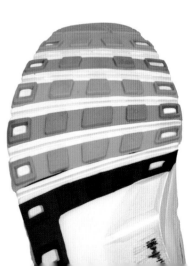

NIKE AIR FOOTSCAPE

A REVOLUTIONARY NEW LACING CONCEPT MADE THIS SHOE A REAL HEAD TURNER.

Enthusiasm for the Air Footscape started off in the East and eventually reached the West as more and more people caught on to the trend. The shoe's tagline read as follows: 'Researched and developed by Nike's advanced product engineering group and Nike sport research lab'. Indeed, the Air Footscape was produced specifically for people with wide feet.

The side lacing system was an innovation and made the shoe look sleek and aerodynamic, regardless of foot size. Several different colourways have been produced over the years, but the original grey / blue is still one of the most coveted.

The ACG (All Condition Gear) variation, produced in Nike Escape colours, also became a hot fashion item – particularly in London, where the release was timed for the autumn / winter 2002 season.

105

AIR FOOTSCAPE

SHOE DATA

FIRST RELEASED
1995
ORIGINAL PURPOSE
Running
EXAMPLE SHOWN
Original
NOTES
The original colours –
grey / blue and the
women's grey / purple –
are still very collectable
and have become
expensive shoes
to source. ■

NIKE **AIR MAX**

IS THAT REAL? CAN I SQUEEZE IT?

AIR MAX

SHOE DATA

FIRST RELEASED
1987
ORIGINAL PURPOSE
Running
EXAMPLE SHOWN
Original
NOTES
The first leather edition
Air Max was released
in 1988. ◼

The Nike Air Max had the Nike Air cushioning
unit on full display. Seeing is believing, and the
transparent window in the rear of the shoe proved
a hit! The sneaker's upper was made of nylon
mesh and synthetic suede.

Since 1987, the Air Max has been produced in
a variety of colourways and fabric combinations,
which have given it a contemporary flavour.
The first reissue was in 1992 and signalled
a change in design: the midsole and outsole used

in this updated version were taken from the Air
Max 3 (now called the Air Max 90). All the shoes
were leather, but in 1995 Nike brought out nylon
reissues. Then in 1996, the swoosh on the side
became smaller.

Nike was experimenting with the formula
at that time. In 2003, two special versions were
created with the help of Japan-based sneaker
specialist store Atmos. The model continues
to evolve to this day.

NIKE **AIR MAX 90**

A MODEL WITH ATTITUDE

The Air Max 90 was referred to as the Air Max or the Air Max III until 2000, when it was reissued. It takes its current name from its launch year, 1990.

The first colourway produced was the men's white / black / cool grey / red. It was striking to say the least: the radiant red around the visible Air window exaggerated the thickness of the midsole, and the matching thermoplastic straps and rubber heel patch added to the overall effect. The upper was made of Duromesh, synthetic suede and synthetic leather. The clean lines and dazzling colours made the Air Max highly sought-after.

In that same year, Nike produced special leather limited edition models in several colourways – the all-black leather model is particularly rare – and there were some truly amazing versions released in 2002. Nike launched an Escape Air Max 90 and a python-inspired edition. Both of these were in high demand by sneaker collectors. This model is especially favoured in Europe.

↑
AIR MAX 93

AIR MAX 90

NIKE **AIR MAX 93**

THE ULTIMATE PROTECTION

The Air Max 93's most talked-about feature was its large 270-degree exposed Nike Air Unit. The Air Sole Unit contained more air and therefore provided greater protection. It was manufactured using a new process called blow moulding, which involved gas being injected through an external tube that forced plastic into the mould. The Air Max 93 was the first to have a coloured Air Unit. Meanwhile, the upper featured a sock-like fit similar to the Air Huarache (page 108).

The model was reissued in 2003. In the same year, Nike produced an Escape-influenced edition and an Air Mowabb (page 118) edition, the latter of which was only available in Europe. Numerous colourways have since been launched worldwide.

AIR MAX 90

SHOE DATA

FIRST RELEASED
1990
ORIGINAL PURPOSE
Running
EXAMPLE SHOWN
Reissue
NOTES
The Air Max 90 was part of Nike's earliest 'Limited Edition' ranges. ◼

107

AIR MAX 93

SHOE DATA

FIRST RELEASED
1993
ORIGINAL PURPOSE
Running
EXAMPLE SHOWN
Original
NOTES
The Air Max 93 used to be called the Air Max 270. ◼

AIR MAX 90 ->

NIKE
AIR HUARACHE

A RUNNING SHOE WITH A LOOK AND FIT LIKE NO OTHER

Its innovative design and fit were incredible: the exposed sock and minimal upper were the only visible technologies. This was called the 'Huarache fit' and was at the heart of the Air Huarache's appeal. The combination of the stretch grip neoprene and Spandex provided a foot-hugging fit. The inspiration for the concept of the 'Huarache fit' came from the old Native American sandal called Huarache. The only Nike branding on the running shoe was the large 'Nike' lettering on the rubber heel strap.

Nike also produced limited edition versions of the Air Huarache in 1992. They came in earth-toned colours with the addition of a nubuck upper, which made this version ideal for the winter climate. This was the last in the series of colourways of the Air Huarache in the 90s. In 2000, the Air Huarache in the original green / royal blue colourway hit the market once more.

108

AIR HUARACHE

SHOE DATA

FIRST RELEASED
1991
ORIGINAL PURPOSE
Running
EXAMPLES SHOWN
Original / Stüssy / Nubuck
NOTES
In 2000, Nike collaborated with clothing company Stüssy to produce two new exciting colour schemes. These two editions have become highly regarded among shoe enthusiasts around the globe. ■

STÜSSY EDITION

NUBUCK EDITION

NIKE
AIR HUARACHE
LIGHT

LOVE IT OR HATE IT, IT WAS CERTAINLY AHEAD OF ITS TIME.

The Nike Air Huarache Light was released in 1993, but its unusual styling made it less popular than the Air Huarache. Some say that this was down to its 'shark-like' features and unusual colourway. The Air Huarache had radiant cool colours, while the vibrant Air Huarache Light was seen as very much the 'ugly duckling'. In fact, the only Huarache characteristic on the Light was the breathable stretch mesh upper. The nylon eyelets and low-profile outsole were unique.

In 2002, the Light was reissued. The timing seems to have been perfect. The original Light wasn't mass-produced like the Air Huarache, and back in 1993 only two colourways were brought out: the men's black / teal / aquamarine and the women's white / purple / blue. The 2002 version was produced in fresh new colourways, which gave the Light a new fan base.

The most interesting editions were special make-ups for the clothing brand Stüssy and Japan-based clothing store Beams. Leather was used on the Stüssy editions. Beams went for a monotone feel with either an all-black or all-grey upper. The most respected colourway, however, remains the original men's black / teal / aquamarine.

NIKE
AIR HUARACHE
TRAINER

THE FIRST CROSS TRAINER TO HAVE THE AIR HUARACHE TECHNOLOGY

A year after the original Air Huarache was introduced, Nike presented the Air Huarache Trainer. This was a cross-training shoe that implemented the 'Huarache fit' and had a large adjustable Velcro strap for added stability. The skeleton frame protected the neoprene and Spandex sock, and the holes in the upper provided great ventilation.

Production of the original Air Huarache Trainer stopped in 1994 but resumed in 2002. A Dominican Republic edition was released in 2003.

AIR HUARACHE TRAINER

SHOE DATA
FIRST RELEASED
1992
ORIGINAL PURPOSE
Running
EXAMPLE SHOWN
Reissue
NOTES
The Air Huarache Trainer was reissued in 2003 in fresh new colourways. ■

AIR HUARACHE LIGHT

SHOE DATA
FIRST RELEASED
1993
ORIGINAL PURPOSE
Running
EXAMPLE SHOWN
Original
NOTES
In 2004, Nike produced a hybrid shoe that was a combination of the Air Huarache Light and another running shoe called the Air Burst. ■

109

NIKE
AIR MAX 95

TAKING SNEAKER DESIGN
TO A NEW LEVEL – AND
THOUGHT BY SOME TO BE THE
GREATEST NIKE SHOE EVER

Designer Sergio Lozano drew inspiration from the human body for the Air Max 95 (or '95s' as most sneakerheads call them): the midsole represents the spine, the graduated panels are the muscle fibres, the loopholes / straps are the ribs, and the mesh is the skin.

The shoe featured minimal branding with the Nike swoosh only making an appearance on the rear side panel. The first colourway released was the black / neon yellow / white, which was like no other Air Max previously produced. The neon yellow helped emphasize the visible Air Units, and the shoe boasted an Air Unit in the forefoot (the front of the shoe). This in itself was something new and exciting, and made the Air Max 95 stand out from the rest of the series.

The technical-looking aesthetics of the upper give the impression of a serious running shoe. The 25 PSI air pressure readings on the Air Units and outsole cemented that impression.

The 95s produced between 1995 and 1996 came in their own specially designed box, with the Air Max 95 logo on the tongue of the shoe. The 95s produced after 1996 do not have the air pressure readings on the Air Units.

One of main reasons for the popularity of the 95s is the number of colourways that have been produced over the years – more than 150 to date. This experimentation with colours and fabrics has kept the 95s alive for avid Air Max enthusiasts.

So far, the upper has been constructed from a range of materials: suede, 3M Scotchlite material, nylon mesh / synthetic leather and premium leather. However, it's not just the upper that has gone through some changes: the outsole and loopholes have all had makeovers too.

111

SHOE DATA

FIRST RELEASED
1995
ORIGINAL PURPOSE
Running
EXAMPLES SHOWN
Originals
NOTES
The Air Max 95 upper
went through a slight
transformation when
Nike added a zip shoelace
cover. This wasn't a good
move, however, and proved
unpopular with consumers.
This version – the Air Max
95z – soon bit the dust. ▨

NIKE
AIR MAX 97

IT LOOKED LIKE
IT HAD BEEN
DESIGNED
BY NASA.

AIR MAX 97

SHOE DATA

FIRST RELEASED
1997
ORIGINAL PURPOSE
Running
EXAMPLE SHOWN
Original
NOTES
The full-length Air
Unit was engineered for
maximum heel-to-toe
impact protection.

Rumour has it that this shoe was originally
going to be called the Air Total Max 3. This
ultra modern-looking Air Max was inspired
by the high-speed Japanese Bullet train.

The sleek liner design and metallic silver
colourway were striking. The full-length visible
Air Unit displayed Nike's Air technology, and
the three reflective lines on the top part of the
shoe provided a space-age 'glow', especially
in the dark.

The 97 was particularly popular in Europe.
The original men's colourway has been reissued
several times over the years. In 2001, a slip-on
version was produced but was frowned upon by
the Air Max 97 purists. The coolest colourway was
the black / neon yellow / metallic silver, which was
released in Japan in 1997.

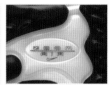

NIKE
AIR ZOOM SPIRIDON

MAXIMUM BRANDING, POWERFUL REFLECTION

This model was one of the first Nike running shoes to incorporate Nike's Air Zoom system, which brings the foot closer to the ground, enhancing performance and providing cushioning. The mesh upper and fish-skin-like swoosh were immediate head turners. Some cool details on the Air Zoom Spiridon included a metallic flip on the midsole and outsole.

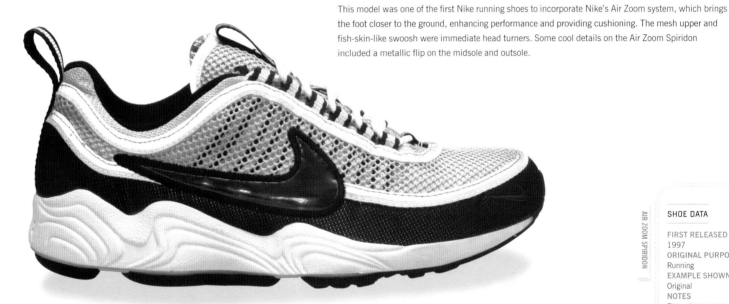

AIR ZOOM SPIRIDON

SHOE DATA

FIRST RELEASED
1997
ORIGINAL PURPOSE
Running
EXAMPLE SHOWN
Original
NOTES
Five colourways were produced. The royal blue / black is the rarest. ■

NIKE
AIR MAX PLUS

THIS STYLISH SNEAKER WAS A FAVOURITE AMONG STREET-CONSCIOUS TEENAGERS.

Over the years, many colour variations of the Air Max Plus were produced for different countries – so much so that it became difficult to keep track of them. The US editions tended to carry lighter colours, while those designed for the Asian market were darker.

Nike realized the popularity of certain colourways and has reissued several. For example, the original 'Hyper Blue' edition has reappeared recently with a slightly different toe-guard, and the original black edition was reissued with patent leather in place of the regular suede areas. Nike has brought out variations on the basic model, including the Air Max Plus 2, 3, 4 and 5, and the slip-on variant of the first model, but none of them were particularly successful.

Although this shoe established itself as a firm favourite in London, where it was associated with the hip-hop and garage scenes, it failed to achieve the same level of success in the US.

The airbrush effect on the upper looked like
a new concept altogether, but the Nike Japan
Terra Rainbow, which came out in 1984, used
a similar fading style. While it was this distinctive
print that got the shoe its initial fan base, later
models of the Air Max Plus featured different
variations on the upper, such as patterned prints
(grid, floral and others), leather and nubuck suede.

AIR MAX PLUS

SHOE DATA

FIRST RELEASED
1998
ORIGINAL PURPOSE
Running
EXAMPLES SHOWN
Originals
NOTES
This model was the
first running shoe to
feature Nike's Tuned
Air system, and the shoe
is often referred to as
the Air TN. The plastic
toe-guard kept things
clean and tidy at the
front end of the shoe.

116

CORTEZ

SHOE DATA

FIRST RELEASED
1972
ORIGINAL PURPOSE
Running
EXAMPLES SHOWN
Original / Reissues
NOTES
The Cortez was worn by
Tom Hanks in the film
Forrest Gump. ■

NIKE **CORTEZ**

ONE OF THE GREAT NIKE SHOES – POPULAR THE WORLD OVER

Originally called the Tiger Corsair, this model was renamed the Cortez in 1972, after the partnership between Nike – known as Blue Ribbon Sports at the time – and Onitsuka Tiger broke down.

Over the years, the Cortez has also undergone several design changes. The original leather model featured a heel pull and was produced in nylon and suede in the 1970s. Nike also released a version for women, the Señorita Cortez, which had a narrow rounded toe-piece and fewer shoelace holes than the regular Cortez. An edition with a leather snake-skin swoosh and Escape models were then released on to the market in the late 1980s. The Cortez was reissued in Europe in the mid-1990s.

In 2003, Nike tried something new using the Internet: the Nike ID system. This gave consumers the opportunity to choose their own Cortez colourway online from a whole range of colour combinations.

NIKE AIR MOWABB

THE BEST NIKE HYBRID
RUNNING / HIKING SHOE

This outdoor training shoe was one of Nike's first ACG models and was a cross between the Air Huarache and the Wildwood (pages 120–121). The speckled midsole gave it a granite look, and its dynamic fitting system was similar to the Huarache fit.

The 1991 editions bore the ACG logo, whereas those produced in 1992 featured the Air Huarache logo. In 1992, Nike also produced Limited Edition models in monotone colourways. The original 1991 colourways remain the most collectable.

SHOE DATA

AIR MOWABB

FIRST RELEASED
1991
ORIGINAL PURPOSE
Outdoor training
EXAMPLE SHOWN
Original
NOTES
An updated version of the Air Mowabb was released in 2003.

118

NIKE AIR STAB

THE TWO 'FORK STABS' IN THE VISIBLE AIR WINDOW GAVE THIS SHOE AN AGGRESSIVE EDGE.

This running shoe featured Nike's Footbridge stability device
in the midsole. The large 'Air Stab' lettering on the
thermoplastic heel counter was there for all to see.
Nike stopped making the Air Stab in spring 1990
to the dismay of many fans.

AIR STAB

SHOE DATA

FIRST RELEASED
1988
ORIGINAL PURPOSE
Running
EXAMPLE SHOWN
Original
NOTES
The Air Stab
was designed by
Tinker Hatfield. ∎

NIKE **WILDWOOD**

BUILT TO LAST IN THE TOUGHEST OUTDOOR ENVIRONMENTS

This is a shoe with attitude! Originally released in 1989, the Wildwood was part of the Nike ACG series. Since its re-release in 1999, the Wildwood has won over a new legion of fans. Its leather instep and tongue, the latter of which bears the ACG logo, keep the foot protected. In 2003, the Wildwood was produced in a multitude of colourways, injecting fresh interest in this model.

120

WILDWOOD

SHOE DATA

FIRST RELEASED
1989
ORIGINAL PURPOSE
Outdoor / Running
EXAMPLE SHOWN
First reissue
NOTES
The Wildwood features the Nike ACG logo, which stands for All Condition Gear. ■

The Air Raid was designed by Tinker Hatfield. The double strap system looked like it was purely cosmetic, but it actually kept the foot very secure. The release of this model coincided with Spike Lee's *Malcolm X*, and the shoe's 'X-look' appearance has led many people to associate the two.

In 1993, the more flamboyant Air Raid II was released. One shoe had a peace sign on the strap and the slogan 'Play Together, Live Together'. The other had a wood-like effect on the midsole and the words 'No Ref, No Wood' on the back.

The Air Raid was reissued in 2003. Five special editions were produced that year: two for the Nike Battleground series and three for the Real Mad Hectic store in Japan. The 1992 Limited Edition model pictured is highly collectable.

NIKE
AIR RAID

YOU EITHER LOVE IT OR HATE IT...

122

AIR RAID

SHOE DATA

FIRST RELEASED
1992
ORIGINAL PURPOSE
Basketball
EXAMPLE SHOWN
Original
NOTES
The Air Raid was initially called the Air Jack before it hit the production line. ■

NIKE
AIR RIFT

A NIGHTCLUB FAVOURITE

The Air Rift was inspired by Kenyan barefoot runners and takes its name from the Rift Valley. The original colours – black / atom red / forest – paid homage to the Kenyan running team. The Air Rift featured an Air Unit in the heel, and the upper was made of synthetic stretch-fit mesh. It is rumoured that the concept came from a Japanese carpenter's shoe.

Up until the late 90s, the Air Rift was available from selected sports shops around the world. In 1999, its appeal widened with the launch of a multitude of colourways including bombay / wash yellow, oxide / blue, and pear / sage.

In 2000, Nike Japan produced a special Brazilian football team edition. This version featured stars and is the most collectable Rift to date. A 'Puerto Rico' edition was released in 2001 to mark the Puerto Rican parade in New York, featuring the country's flag on the Velcro strap.

The Air Rift has also gone through several cosmetic changes, including the use of leather and suede on the upper. In 2002, Nike released a mid-cut version called the Air Rift Cover – a higher version of the Air Rift, with the cut-out hole covered over – but it wasn't as popular as the original.

AIR RIFT

123

SHOE DATA

FIRST RELEASED
1995
ORIGINAL PURPOSE
Running
EXAMPLE SHOWN
Original
NOTES
Oscar-winning actress Halle Berry designed an Air Rift for Nike as part of the Nike Artist series in 2003.

NIKE LDV

ONE OF THE FIRST RUNNING SHOES TO BOAST A BREATHABLE MESH UPPER.

SHOE DATA

LDV

FIRST RELEASED
1978
ORIGINAL PURPOSE
Running
EXAMPLE SHOWN
Reissue
NOTES
L and D in LDV stand
for long distance. ■

This long-distance running shoe bore similarities to the Nike Elite. Its aggressive-looking waffle outsole had a large stud-like pattern which was ideal for off-road running. A more refined version of the LDV was reissued in 1999. The mesh upper had disappeared, replaced by leather in diverse colourways. In Japan, Nike released Guam-inspired versions but they were not launched globally. The original issues are still considered the finest by collectors.

NIKE DAYBREAK

A SNEAKER THAT REFLECTS ITS INSPIRATION: THE DAYBREAK

The Nike Daybreak had superior cushioning and a thick flared EVA midsole. It looked almost identical to the LDV, apart from its nylon upper. It also had a cup innersole in order to raise the foot, and extra padding on the shoe collar. This shoe has yet to be reissued.

DAYBREAK

SHOE DATA

FIRST RELEASED
1979
ORIGINAL PURPOSE
Running
EXAMPLE SHOWN
Original
NOTES
It was manufactured mainly in the US.

NIKE **AIR 180**

AN UNDERRATED CLASSIC

In spring 1991, the Nike Air 180 was released. This revolutionary
shoe contained fifty per cent more air than previous Air Max models.
Nike went one step further by displaying this technology through a visible
protective outsole. The Air 180 was only around for a year, even though
Nike supported its launch with a huge TV advertising campaign involving
high-profile filmmakers and directors.

During 1991–92, a variety of colourways
were produced. The most desirable colours
out there are the original men's colour and the
Europe-only women's white / crimson / magenta
(pictured). The Olympic Air Force 180 is regarded
as the best Air 180 shoe ever.

SHOE DATA

FIRST RELEASED
1991
ORIGINAL PURPOSE
Running
EXAMPLE SHOWN
Original
NOTES
The low-cut version of
the Air Force 180 was
worn by NBA star Charles
Barkley at the 1992
Barcelona Olympics. ■

AIR 180

AIR PRESTO

SHOE DATA

FIRST RELEASED
2000
ORIGINAL PURPOSE
Running
EXAMPLES SHOWN
Originals
NOTES
With more colourways
than ever before,
it isn't hard to see
why the Air Presto is an
extremely popular shoe. ■

NIKE
AIR PRESTO

**THEY CALLED IT
THE 'T-SHIRT FOR
YOUR FEET'.**

This sneaker didn't come in conventional
shoe sizes. It had a similar sizing structure
to that of a T-shirt: XS, S, M, L, XL and XXL.
Its lightweight stretch-mesh upper, with
the addition of the support cage, provided
a comfortable fit. Nike experimented with
various upper fabrics including velour.

NIKE SHOX R4

BOING, BOING, BOING

SHOX R4

SHOE DATA

FIRST RELEASED
2000
ORIGINAL PURPOSE
Running
EXAMPLE SHOWN
Original
NOTES
Bruce Kilgore and Sergio
Lozano designed the Shox
R4. Kilgore was the man
behind the Air Force 1
and the Air 180. ■

The experts at the Nike lab worked on the Shox technology for sixteen years. In 2000, it was finally revealed to the world. Three editions were released: the Shox R4, BB4 and XTR.

How did they work? The principle is simple – the Shox technology absorbs energy from the impact of the wearer's 'heel strike' and returns it to the wearer as he or she transfers weight forward to 'toe-off' on to the next stride. The Shox technology is cutting edge, using high-density PU foam columns as the 'shock absorbers' with a TPU heel counter to ensure even distribution of the impact energy. Do they work? We'll let you decide for yourselves.

The R4 running shoe has been the most successful. The track-inspired look of the upper was complemented by the futuristic technology in the rear. It has been produced in a variety of colours and was also available on Nike ID. A special European edition was released in 2003. The R4 is the only model out of the original three to have been released in an array of different colourways.

NIKE AIR EPIC

THIS WAS CONSIDERED A STATE-OF-THE-ART SHOE IN THE MID-1980s.

The Air Epic featured a full-length Air midsole (similar to the Air Tailwind) and the Air Wedge, a stabilizing device. It was re-released in 2003, with just one small change: the 'Air' on the heel patch was replaced with 'Nike'.

A special edition was produced for a London-based store called Foot Patrol. It had the store's colourway and featured local details such as a London taxi on the tongue.

AIR EPIC

SHOE DATA

FIRST RELEASED
1985
ORIGINAL PURPOSE
Running
EXAMPLES SHOWN
Reissue / Foot Patrol
NOTES
The Air Epic was one of the last Nike shoes to be made in the US. ■

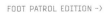

FOOT PATROL EDITION ->

The upper on The Sting was made of soft, thin, rust-coloured suede, and nylon was used on the side panels. It was one of the first running shoes to use the D-ring eyelets and boasted a suction outsole. The Sting was reissued in 2003 in new colourways.

130

NIKE THE STING
LOW PROFILE BUT LONG DISTANCE

THE STING

SHOE DATA

FIRST RELEASED
1978
ORIGINAL PURPOSE
Running
EXAMPLE SHOWN
Reissue
NOTES
An improved model of The Sting was released in the late 1970s. It had fewer D-rings and laceholes and also had a flared outsole.

NIKE
WINDRUNNER

AN AWESOME SHOE WITH A COOL PRICE TAG

The Nike Windrunner was a running shoe for the casual wearer. Over the years, Nike has added various unique features such as imitation elephant-skin prints, a nubuck upper and nylon / mesh combinations.

Nike ceased producing the Windrunner in the early 1990s. It was reissued in 1999 in new colourways. Special Nike Co.Jp models were released a few years later.

131

WINDRUNNER

SHOE DATA

FIRST RELEASED
1987
ORIGINAL PURPOSE
Running
EXAMPLE SHOWN
Original
NOTES
Nike released an Escape edition in 1989.

NIKE **LAHAR**

THE SON OF LAVA DOME'S BIG BROTHER

This high-top outdoor trekking shoe had a tough suede and nylon upper, and its chunky outsole was invincible. 'Lahar' was printed on the innersole.

Between 1988 and 1989, Nike released Escape editions of this model. They were constructed from all-leather or all-nubuck and are well respected.

SHOE DATA

LAHAR

FIRST RELEASED
1987
ORIGINAL PURPOSE
Trekking
EXAMPLE SHOWN
Escape edition
NOTES
The Escape edition was the first shoe in Nike's Limited Edition series. ◼

NIKE

ONE OF NIKE'S FIRST ATTEMPTS AT A SEMI-RUNNING AND TREKKING SHOE

Made of breathable mesh and reinforced suede or leather overlays, with a rubber toe-guard, chunky outsole and two-toned upper, the Lava Dome was difficult to beat. Later models had ACG on the innersole.

Nike produced a Lady Lava Dome in 2000. A similar-looking high-top version was called the Approach.

NIKE LAVA FLOW

THE WILDWOOD WAS A NATURAL PROGRESSION FROM THE LAVA FLOW...

The Lava Flow was a refined version of the Lava Dome. It was a great outdoor shoe and came in some fantastic colourways with fluorescent hiking shoelaces. The Lava Flow was made in 1989, but it had disappeared from the market by the end of 1990.

LAVA FLOW

SHOE DATA

FIRST RELEASED
1989
ORIGINAL PURPOSE
Trekking
EXAMPLE SHOWN
Original
NOTES
The high-top version of the Lava Flow was called the Baltora. ▪

133

LAVA DOME

SHOE DATA

FIRST RELEASED
1981
ORIGINAL PURPOSE
Trekking
EXAMPLE SHOWN
Reissue
NOTES
The Lava Dome was the start of Nike's exploration of outdoor footwear and products. ▪

134

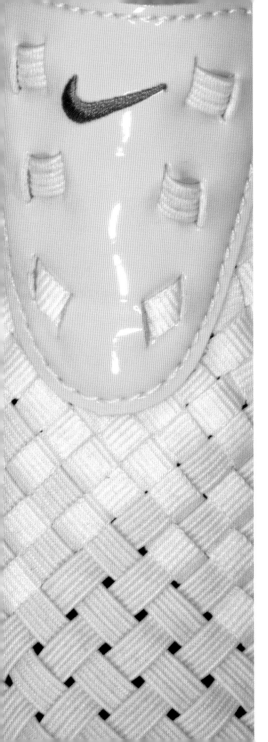

THE AIR WOVEN WAS INITIALLY WHAT NIKE REFERS TO AS A STEPCHILD: A PROTOTYPE THAT DIDN'T MAKE THE PRODUCTION LINE.

The lack of foot support and the fragility of its upper section made this shoe less functional than most others in Nike's range. The Woven was initially launched in Japan and rolled out to New York and London, where it sold out almost immediately.

As it was a hand-made item, the shoe was only produced in small numbers. The Woven's material was created by weaving nylon (for strength) and rubber (for stretch). The fit of the shoe is unique, as the upper is made up of many pieces (rather than just one or two pieces), and there is also Zoom Air technology in the heel of the shoe. One of the most collectable shoes, the early colourways have become highly sought-after.

WOVEN

SHOE DATA

FIRST RELEASED
2000
ORIGINAL PURPOSE
Lifestyle
EXAMPLES SHOWN
Originals
NOTES
The Air Woven was designed by Mike Aveni, who has been part of the development of Nike's running series for over a decade. ■

NIKE **AIR TECH CHALLENGE IV**

OTHERWISE KNOWN AS THE 'AGASSI', THIS WAS THE
SIGNATURE MODEL OF THE TENNIS STAR.

SHOE DATA

FIRST RELEASED
1991
ORIGINAL PURPOSE
Tennis
EXAMPLE SHOWN
Original
NOTES
This style of airbrush
colouring was included
on the Andre Agassi Nike
clothing line. ■

AIR TECH CHALLENGE IV

There have been various models of this fourth
edition of the Air Tech Challenge, which was
released in 1991, but this one was by far the most
appealing. Its splash of tie-dye on the back panels
and airbrushed midsole were not what you might
expect from a tennis shoe.

The Air Tech Challenge IV also had a visible
air window in the airbrushed midsole. 'Nike'
decorated the side panels instead of the
usual swoosh.

It was reissued in 2000 in one colourway.
Mid-cut and low-cut versions of this shoe were
also brought out.

NIKE **CHALLENGE COURT**

AT FIRST GLANCE, IT'S NOT CLEAR WHAT THIS SNEAKER
WAS DESIGNED FOR.

This shoe was considered quite remarkable when
it was launched. It had a multifunctional design,
which made it suitable for an array of sports
including basketball and tennis.

Its upper was made of nylon mesh and full-grain
leather, and the extended ankle collar offered
good support. The Challenge Court was reissued
in 2003 in the original white / blue / red, and in
2004 a low-cut edition was produced. The most
sought-after edition is the 1984 white / burgundy
colourway, which featured a gum outsole.

CHALLENGE COURT

SHOE DATA

FIRST RELEASED
1984
ORIGINAL PURPOSE
Racketball / Tennis
EXAMPLE SHOWN
Original
NOTES
John McEnroe was wearing
the Challenge Court when
he won the Davis Cup,
the Australian Indoor
Championship, and
the Grand Prix
Tournament in Tokyo. ■

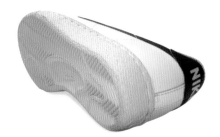

NIKE **BRUIN**

ONE OF NIKE'S EARLIEST LOW-TOP BASKETBALL SHOES

The first Bruin was made in 1972 and featured the classic herringbone-design outsole. Nike created this model in a variety of colours in both suede and leather.

  Like the Blazer, the Bruin has played an important part in Nike's basketball shoe history. It also featured the larger fat belly swoosh, which Nike designers reduced in size in 1980.

BRUIN

SHOE DATA

FIRST RELEASED
1972
ORIGINAL PURPOSE
Basketball
EXAMPLE SHOWN
Original
NOTES
This model was worn by Michael J. Fox in the film *Back to the Future.* ▪

↑
STÜSSY EDITIONS

NIKE BLAZER

THE SWOOSH STOOD OUT
IN A BLAZE OF GLORY.

The Nike designers wanted the swoosh on this model to be really big so that everybody would notice it. The Blazer was worn and represented by basketball legend George Gervin, aka the Ice Man. The Blazer didn't have great technology, but the process of fusing the outsole to the upper was pretty extreme – it was executed with an autoclave, which baked the shoes at a high temperature. This melded the upper to the midsole. Blazers were produced in leather, suede and canvas.

In 2001, Nike collaborated with streetwear label Stüssy to produce two special colourways. In 2003, it continued with the 'street' theme when it worked with New York graffiti artist Futura as part of Nike's Artist series. These are now hot collectors' items – only 1,000 pairs were ever produced.

BLAZER

SHOE DATA

FIRST RELEASED
1972
ORIGINAL PURPOSE
Basketball
EXAMPLES SHOWN
Reissue / Stüssy editions
NOTES
The canvas version of the Blazer was called the All Court. ▪

NIKE
DUNK

A NEAR ENDLESS MYRIAD OF COLOURWAYS FOR YOUR FAVOURITE COLLEGE TEAM

Before the NBA courts were blessed with the Nike Air Jordan I, the Nike Dunk fitted the bill. The Dunk has been around since 1985, and it has been brought out in a multitude of basketball team colourways. It was worn during the NCAA basketball tournaments of 1985–86 by universities such as Syracuse, Michigan, Maryland, UNLV and Arizona.

The Dunk could be coordinated with any team basketball kit. It came with two different coloured sets of laces and a matching shoebox, and it was one of the original catalysts of the colourway explosion.

The original Dunk was – and still is – one of the most prized possessions for a sneaker connoisseur. High demand influenced Nike's decision to reissue the model in 1998, since when there have been many new colourways. Special collaborations and regional releases have made the Dunk stronger than ever.

140

SHOE DATA

FIRST RELEASED
1985
ORIGINAL PURPOSE
Basketball
EXAMPLES SHOWN
Originals / Reissues
NOTES
In 1999, Nike released the skate Dunk, which featured a padded tongue and ankle collar. In 2004, Nike released the first Dunk mid. ■

DUNK

↑
SUPREME EDITION

SUPREME COLLABORATION
Nike collaborated with New York skate brand Supreme in 2002 to produce the Supreme Dunk range. Taking inspiration from the Nike Air Jordan III, this model looked amazing and consequently became the most sought-after Dunk.

In 2003, Supreme reworked a high-top version of the Dunk into three team colourways and added nice details such as a nameplate-inspired Supreme lace jewel, star-printed and crocodile-skin textured leather, and three sets of laces.

NIKE LEGEND

LEGEND BY NAME, LEGEND BY NATURE

The Nike Legend was produced for heavyweight basketball players. It featured Nike's trademark variable width lacing system, which was used on the brand's advanced running shoes during the 1980s. The Legend came in a low- and high-top edition: the high top had a hinged eyelet design, which helped the top part of the shoe around the ankle support to bend instead of buckling. This prevented the ankle support from flexing and digging into the wearer's ankle.

The Legend was one of the first Nike basketball shoes to feature a perforated toe area, which kept the wearer's foot as cool as possible. Retired NBA superstar Patrick Ewing wore the Legend high-top edition when playing for the Georgetown Hoyas in the NCAA league. Maybe one day the Legend will return…

142

LEGEND

SHOE DATA

FIRST RELEASED
1983
ORIGINAL PURPOSE
Basketball
EXAMPLE SHOWN
Original
NOTES
The Legend was one of the first Nike basketball shoes to feature a coloured outsole. ◼

NIKE DYNASTY

CONTINUING THE LINE...

Nike produced the Dynasty High in 1985. It had similar characteristics to other Nike basketball shoes at that time. For example, it had the same ankle support strap as the Air Force 1 (pages 146–147) and the same outsole as the Penetrator.

The use of colour on the Nike Dynasty resembled that on the Dunk, with the matching perforated toe box and swoosh. 'Nike' lettering on the ankle completes the look. If you have a pair, keep hold of them: this is a particularly rare Nike product.

DYNASTY

SHOE DATA

FIRST RELEASED
1985
ORIGINAL PURPOSE
Basketball
EXAMPLE SHOWN
Original
NOTES
The Nike Georgetown was virtually the same as the Dynasty but was entirely white and had 'Nike' printed on the rear. ■

NIKE VANDAL

AS FEATURED IN THE ROCK STEADY CREW'S UPROCK MUSIC VIDEO...

The Nike Vandal was made from 1984 until 1987. Its upper was made of thick canvas or nylon, rather than leather. The nylon editions were called Vandal Supreme and came with two different coloured sets of laces and a Velcro ankle support strap (with a three-way colour scheme).

The Vandal was one of the first fashionable basketball shoes. In 2003, the Vandal and Vandal Supreme returned. That year, an assortment of special editions were launched: the Jim Morrison, the Haight Street and the Geoff McFetridge. In 2004, camouflage and Premium editions were produced.

The original Vandals are rare gems: they ooze quality and look great. The reissues were not produced to the original spec, and sneaker fans tend to prefer the real thing.

144

VANDAL

SHOE DATA

FIRST RELEASED
1984
ORIGINAL PURPOSE
Basketball
EXAMPLE SHOWN
Original
NOTES
The Nike Vandal had a cameo appearance in the film *Terminator*. ▪

PREMIUM EDITION

NIKE TERMINATOR

ANYTHING IN GEORGETOWN COLOURS IS RESPECTED BY THE SERIOUS COLLECTOR.

The Terminator was produced as a team shoe for the Georgetown Hoyas university basketball team. It was made in their team colours of navy and grey, and it was a cross between the Nike Legend and the Big Nike. It had a large 'Nike' printed on the heel, although the Georgetown Hoyas had 'Hoyas' printed on their shoes instead of the regular Nike.

The Terminator was subsequently produced in other colourways, and canvas was used on the toe box and side panels. These were produced in high and low tops.

The original Terminator is well respected by most sneaker connoisseurs and has sold for considerable sums. Nike reissued the original Hoyas-coloured Terminator in 2003.

TERMINATOR

SHOE DATA

FIRST RELEASED
1985
ORIGINAL PURPOSE
Basketball
EXAMPLES SHOWN
Reissue / Premium
NOTES
The Grunge Terminator was released in 2004.

STASH COLLABORATION

YEAR OF THE HORSE EDITION

BLACK SNAKE-SKIN EDITION

HTM EDITION

WEST INDIES EDITION

146

SHOE DATA

FIRST RELEASED
1982
ORIGINAL PURPOSE
Basketball
EXAMPLES SHOWN
Reissues
NOTES
The correct name for
the ankle strap is the
Proprioceptus Belt. ◼

AIR FORCE 1

NIKE
AIR FORCE 1

THIS HAS TO BE
ONE OF NIKE'S MOST
RECOGNIZABLE BASKETBALL
SILHOUETTES.

NELLYVILLE EDITION

SHEED EDITION

EMERALD GREEN MID EDITION

LASER EDITION

PUERTO RICO EDITION

The original version of this model was inspired by hiking shoes, but it has exceeded all expectations. It didn't have a perforated toe box but did feature a mesh side panel. As well as being the most functional basketball shoe at that time, it was the first Nike basketball shoe to feature the full-length Nike Air Sole.

Some people saw the strap as a mere fashion accessory, but it played an extremely important role. The strap made the fit secure and was used to prevent ankle injury. At first this model was only produced in a high and a low; the mid version was produced later.

The Air Force 1 has become popular on the hip-hop scene, partly owing to the huge range of colourways that have been produced over the years. There have also been numerous limited edition collaborative models – from Puerto Rico to Los Angeles – and countless colourway variations.

NIKE **AIR JORDAN I**

THE BLACK / RED COLOURWAY — THE FIRST NIKE AIR JORDAN COLOURWAY WORN BY MICHAEL JORDAN — DEMANDED YOUR FULL ATTENTION.

This model was produced for basketball pro Michael Jordan, and its launch started off a whole generation of Air Jordan shoes. The red / black colourway broke the NBA league colour rules, and the shoes were banned. Michael only wore the red / black three times, but the ban actually fuelled Air Jordan mania. Nike put together a new colourway, which included more white. The winged basketball logo was there to stay!

AIR JORDAN II

The Nike Air Jordan II was released in 1986. It was the only Air Jordan that did not get produced in black, and Nike released both high- and low-top versions.

It was more refined and, some say, more stylized than the first edition. Maybe this was because it was manufactured in Italy.

Michael Jordan scored sixty-one points in one game wearing this shoe. In that same year he played in the NBA All Star game and won the Slam Dunk competition.

The Air Jordan II did not have the Nike swoosh, which was unusual for the time. It has been reissued twice by popular demand.

AIR JORDAN III

The Nike Air Jordan III was released in 1988. The winged logo had gone, and the Jumpman was born – the new logo that is now associated with Jordan.

This model featured elephant-print leather around the toe and heel area. The Air Jordan III, like the II, was swoosh-less. However, the back of the shoe made up for it: it had a sizeable plastic, transparent heel counter with 'Nike Air' in large letters. The Air Jordan III was reissued in 1990 and 2001.

148

AIR JORDAN I

SHOE DATA

FIRST RELEASED
1985
ORIGINAL PURPOSE
Basketball
EXAMPLES SHOWN
Originals
NOTES
Jordan wore Converse
and adidas before signing
with Nike. ■

AIR JORDAN IV

The Nike Air Jordan IV was released in 1989. This was one of the most popular Air Jordans ever, selling out the minute it hit the stores.

It had similarities to the Air Jordan III. The upper on this Jordan was made of synthetic leather, and there was a toggle to ease lacing.

It was reissued in 1999, and two new editions – Retro Plus – were produced. The Jumpman was used on the heel instead of the 'Nike Air'.

AIR JORDAN V

The Nike Air Jordan V was originally released in 1990. The inspiration for the design of this shoe came from the World War II Mustang fighter aeroplane. The Jumpman made two appearances on this model: on the reflective tongue and underneath on the translucent outsole. Air Jordan V was reissued in 2000.

NIKE
AIR ALPHA FORCE II

'SIR CHARLES' WAS A FORCE TO BE RECKONED WITH, AND SO WERE HIS SHOES.

This model was worn by the legendary Charles Barkley. The Velcro strap at the front of the shoe distinguished the Air Alpha Force II from other Nike basketball shoes at that time. The wide outsole was similar to that of the Air Force III.

In 2004, the Air Alpha Force II returned. One of the most exciting colourways was the sport red / college navy / pearl grey, which was part of Nike's Rewind series. This series was produced in NBA team colourways. The holy grail of Air Alpha Force IIs is the 1988 Escape Limited Edition.

SHOE DATA

AIR ALPHA FORCE II

FIRST RELEASED
1988
ORIGINAL PURPOSE
Basketball
EXAMPLES SHOWN
Originals
NOTES
Michael Jordan wore the Air Alpha Force in 1986. ■

NIKE AIR PRESSURE

EVERYBODY THINKS THAT THESE ARE THE SHOES IN *BACK TO THE FUTURE II.*

The Air Pressure marked a turning point for Nike: the use of air in the chambers inside the ankle support to achieve a custom fit. Air was pumped into them with an inflatable hand-pump device that came with the shoes. The more air, the tighter the fit. A valve on the back of the shoe was used to release the air. The Air Pressure was only produced for one year.

AIR PRESSURE

SHOE DATA

FIRST RELEASED
1989
ORIGINAL PURPOSE
Basketball
EXAMPLE SHOWN
Original
NOTES
Air Pressures came
in their own plastic box. ■

**NIKE
AIR TRAINER 1**

THE CROSS-TRAINING
REVOLUTION STARTS HERE.

Nike designer Tinker Hatfield produced the first athletic cross-training shoe. Hatfield was watching athletes train at his local gym and he could see that they were using two different pairs of shoes: one for running and another for weight training. This gave him the idea for a multipurpose shoe.

The Air Trainer was a huge success when it was launched in 1987. Nike went on to develop more technical Air Trainers over the years. The original was reissued in the mid-1990s, and since then this model has been produced in a multitude of new colourways. In 2003, Nike created a special skate edition.

⌃
SKATE EDITION

AIR TRAINER 1

SHOE DATA

FIRST RELEASED
1987
ORIGINAL PURPOSE
Cross-training
EXAMPLES SHOWN
Reissues / Skate
NOTES
The Air Trainer was worn by tennis superstar John McEnroe and also made an appearance in the NBA. ◼

NIKE WIMBLEDON

THE LARGE SKY-BLUE SWOOSH WAS A BIG PART OF THE ATTRACTION.

This was one of Nike's most successful tennis shoes. Its sales were bolstered by John McEnroe, who used to wear the Wimbledon.

Nike gave the Wimbledon a makeover in 1985: the outsole became thinner, and the swoosh was reduced in size. The old Nike lettering and orange swoosh were gone. A variety of Wimbledon-inspired shoes were launched over the years, but this 1985 edition was the most memorable. Nike stopped producing the Wimbledon in 1986, only to reissue it in the new millennium.

SHOE DATA

FIRST RELEASED
1982
ORIGINAL PURPOSE
Tennis
EXAMPLES SHOWN
Originals
NOTES
Nike reissued the Wimbledon in 2002. ■

WIMBLEDON

ONITSUKA TIGER

In 1949, Japanese entrepreneur Kihachiro Onitsuka founded Onitsuka Co. Ltd, the company destined to become world-renowned sports brand ASICS. Encouraged by a coach in his home town of Kobe, Onitsuka brought out the first Japanese-made basketball shoes at a time when there were no other specialist sports shoe makers in Japan. His first design looked more like a straw sandal than a basketball shoe, but Onitsuka worked hard to research the sport by observing the players' movements – a key factor in Onitsuka's future success.

A flash of inspiration came in 1951 when he realized that the key to success could lie in the 'sucking discs' of an octopus tentacle. After Onitsuka had finished his first basketball shoe, the product's reputation spread so quickly that soon, it is claimed, he took a fifty per cent share of Japan's sports shoe market.

Onitsuka went on to purchase the Tiger brand in 1958. When he saw Ethiopian athlete Abebe Bikila win the 1960 Olympic marathon in Rome barefoot, Onitsuka turned the situation to his own advantage by persuading the gold medallist to wear his brand for the Mainichi marathon in Japan. Needless to say, Bikila won.

A whole host of other running stars have become associated with the brand over the years, including Kenji Kimihara, Derek Crayton, Lasse Viren, Toru Terasawa, Yuko Arimori and Naoko Takahashi.

Onitsuka Tiger has appeared in many great movie moments as well as victories on the running track – Bruce Lee is forever associated with the brand (see the Mexico on page 158), and more recently Uma Thurman went out seeking revenge in *Kill Bill* in her Onitsuka Tiger Tai Chis (page 159), which has brought the brand to people's attention once more. There aren't many brands which can boast of such performance-enhancing designs and cult appeal in equal measure.

The company expanded into sports apparel when, in 1976, it finalized a deal with sportswear manufacturer GTO and knitwear firm Jelenk. The three companies merged the following year to form ASICS. It now claims to rank among the top five largest companies in the sports shoe industry. Never one to rest on his laurels, in 1999 Onitsuka is reported to have said: 'This first half century was only the beginning.'

ONITSUKA TIGER **MEXICO**
THE FIRST SHOE IN THE RANGE TO FEATURE THE TIGER STRIPES ON THE SIDE PANEL.

MEXICO

The Mexico has been released in various colours over the years. It was the first model to feature the stripes on the side of the upper section. However, they served a greater need than mere aesthetics. Known as Tiger stripes, they are specifically designed to add support to the foot whilst running.

The extremely lightweight leather upper made this shoe ideal for sprinting. In fact, it was first endorsed by the Japanese athletics team at the 1968 Olympic Games. The suede toe piece added durability to what was a clean and simple model in the Onitsuka range.

SHOE DATA

FIRST RELEASED
1966
ORIGINAL PURPOSE
Running
EXAMPLES SHOWN
Reissues
NOTES
The Mexico is infamous for being worn by Bruce Lee in his film *Game of Death* in 1978, which also starred Kareem Abdul-Jabbar. ▮

ONITSUKA TIGER **TAI CHI**

A MOVIE STAR IN THE MAKING...

With its effortless style, the Tai Chi has become a favourite among
martial arts experts. It is particularly noted for being the shoe worn
by actress Uma Thurman in Quentin Tarantino's 2003 film *Kill Bill*.
 Although it is extremely lightweight, it offers tremendous strength.
Its lack of midsole enables heightened control of the sole,
making it especially flexible and a must for any balance-
orientated sports.

SHOE DATA

FIRST PRODUCED
1960s–1970s
ORIGINAL PURPOSE
Training
EXAMPLE SHOWN
Reissue
NOTES
The Onitsuka Tai Chi
has become a very
fashionable model,
successfully bridging
function and style. ■

ONITSUKA TIGER
ULTIMATE 81

A TECHNICAL HEAVYWEIGHT

ULTIMATE 81

SHOE DATA

FIRST RELEASED
1981
ORIGINAL PURPOSE
Running
EXAMPLES SHOWN
Originals
NOTES
In 2002, Onitsuka
Tiger released a suede
version called the
Ultimate 81 SD. ■

This strikingly lightweight shoe was designed with heel stability in mind. The upper was made of synthetic leather and mesh, while the wrap-around outsole provided great traction on the road. It was reissued in 2002 as the Ultimate 81 SD.

ONITSUKA TIGER
TUG OF WAR

THE ONLY TUG OF
WAR SHOE FROM
A SPORTS BRAND

Designed for the competitive sport of tug of war,
the key to its design lay in the outsole, which had
amazing grip.

SHOE DATA

FIRST RELEASED
1982
ORIGINAL PURPOSE
Tug of war
EXAMPLE SHOWN
Reissue
NOTES
Various colourways
have been produced
over the years. ▇

ONITSUKA TIGER
FABRE

A TRUE BASKETBALL FAN

Fabre is an abbreviation of the basketball term 'fast break', referring to a particular manoeuvre through which a team changes strategy quickly and aggressively from defence to offence. In the mid-1980s, when the Fabre was released, it was at the cutting edge of technology. It was the sports shoe of choice for many top NBA and international basketball stars. The Fabre's particular selling point lay in its unique 'sticky sole', which was designed to give players extra grip and mobility on the basketball court.

This model's simple design has enabled it to retain a stylish look even in today's highly competitive market. The suede upper and unmistakable Tiger stripes have given it the edge over many other competitors who have re-released old models.

FABRE

SHOE DATA

FIRST RELEASED
1985
ORIGINAL PURPOSE
Basketball
EXAMPLE SHOWN
Original
NOTES
The Fabre shoe takes its name from the fast break basketball move. ■

PONY

PONY

Founded in 1972 by Roberto Mueller, Pony soon became one of the most important athletic brands in the world. Renowned for being at the forefront of technological innovation, Pony also benefited from celebrity endorsement. By the late 1970s, many top NBA basketball players were wearing Pony's chevron design, but sporting legends from other disciplines have also been associated with the brand, including boxer Muhammad Ali.

Certainly in the early days, Pony was a little-known brand outside the US. However, that all changed with the release of the Linebacker model (pages 166–167). Nowadays, the Pony brand is more often associated with fashion than sports – an image that has been cemented with The One and Only collection, the brand's 2004 fashion deal with music icon Snoop Dogg.

In 2003, Global Brand Marketing Inc., the owner of Dry-shoD shoes and Global Feet retail store, and the global footwear licensee of Diesel, XOXO, Nautica and Mecca, acquired a majority share of Pony International, the company that owns the brand, from entertainment talent agency The Firm. The future certainly looks bright for Pony.

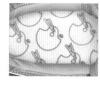
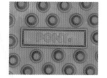

PONY
LINEBACKER

THIS SHOE BROUGHT
AMERICAN FOOTBALL FANS
A FEW YARDS CLOSER TO
THEIR IDOLS.

At a time when global awareness of American football was soaring – especially in the UK where it was shown regularly on TV – Pony made its own impact with the launch of the Linebacker. The shoe was endorsed by the NFL and came in all the major team colours.

Although it was only a replica of the sneakers worn by the players on the field, it was promoted as street fashion with the slogan 'Pound the streets, touch the sky'. Every child fan had a pair in his or her team's colourway.

The Miami Dolphins, with their orange and turquoise, had one of the most striking shoes in the range. The design incorporated suede and mesh, with the fold-over tongue and studs on the outsole, which were a tradition of the game.

↑
CRICKET EDITION

LINEBACKER

SHOE DATA

FIRST RELEASED
1983
ORIGINAL PURPOSE
American football
EXAMPLES SHOWN
Originals / Cricket
NOTES
Pony also released
a spin-off shoe called
the Cricket, which was
virtually the same as the
original. It featured leather
and had cricket bats on
the innersole. ■

PONY
CITY WINGS

BASKETBALL LEGEND SPUD WEBB FLEW
WITH CITY WINGS IN 1986.

SHOE DATA

FIRST PRODUCED
1980s
ORIGINAL PURPOSE
Basketball
EXAMPLE SHOWN
Reissue
NOTES
Spud Webb made his
mark with NC State in
the NCAA and the Atlanta
Hawks in the NBA.

Pony produced both high- and low-top versions
of City Wings in a variety of different colour
combinations. The body of the shoe was made
of fine leather with coloured shoe laces and toe
box. The telltale pony chevron adorned the side
of the sneaker, enhanced by the striking City
Wings logo on the tongue. The high-top
version also featured the logo on the ankle
support. City Wings was reissued in 2003.

SHOE DATA

FIRST PRODUCED
1980s
ORIGINAL PURPOSE
Basketball
EXAMPLES SHOWN
Reissues
NOTES
Pony was one of the
first brands to use mesh
on the uppers of its
basketball shoes. ■

PONY
UPTOWN / MIDTOWN

**THE CHEVRON MADE IT
DIFFICULT TO MISS.**

First released in the mid-80s, the Uptown
also came in a low-top version called the
Midtown. Available in both leather and in
polyester mesh with leather trimmings,
the two models boasted a variety
of colourways.

The sneakers were given a new look in
2004 when Pony reissued both models
in fresh, up-to-date colourways.

PONY TOP STAR

IT OFFERED MORE COLOURWAYS THAN ANY PONY SHOE BEFORE IT.

Designed for basketball, the original 1970s editions of the Top Star came in either suede or leather and featured team colourways. High- and low-top versions were produced.

A real favourite among NBA superstars of the time, the Top Star was reissued in 2004 to appeal to a new generation of basketball fans.

SHOE DATA

TOP STAR

FIRST PRODUCED
1970s
ORIGINAL PURPOSE
Basketball
EXAMPLES SHOWN
Reissues
NOTES
The Top Star was worn by NBA superstars Bob McAdoo, John Havlicek and Paul Silas. ▪

OTHER INTERESTING MODELS

FOREST HILLS ->

LADY ANHEIM ->

ROSCOE ->

PONY TRACY AUSTIN

PEOPLE OFTEN FORGET THAT PONY MADE GREAT TENNIS SHOES.

Named after the tennis ace who – at sixteen – became the youngest player to win the US Open in 1979, the Pony Tracy Austin featured a nylon mesh upper with leather trimmings. The sneaker's baby-blue chevron along the side matched its nubbed outsole, and Austin's autograph was emblazoned on the back.

Austin was extremely gifted and was awarded 'Female Athlete of the Year' status by the Associated Press in both 1979 and 1981. However, she was plagued by neck and back injuries, which shortened her career dramatically after 1983. This turn of events did not bode well for the Tracy Austin sneaker, which was only produced for one year.

TRACY AUSTIN

SHOE DATA

FIRST PRODUCED
1980s
ORIGINAL PURPOSE
Tennis
EXAMPLES SHOWN
Originals
NOTES
Tracy Austin was ranked among the top ten in the world and she became the youngest woman ever to represent the US in the Wightman and Federation Cups. ■

PRO-KEDS

In 1892, nine small rubber factories merged to form the U. S. Rubber Company. Among them was Connecticut-based Goodyear Metallic Rubber Shoe Company, which was the first licensee of vulcanization – an innovative manufacturing process of hardening rubber by using sulphur at high temperatures. This process enabled the U. S. Rubber Company to produce what is said to be the world's first sneaker: a rubber-soled shoe called the Keds, which was named in 1916 and mass-marketed from 1917 onwards.

In 1949, a new athletic footwear line was brought out under the Keds brand, targeting basketball players in particular: PRO-Keds. The first product was the classic Royal (page 176), a canvas basketball shoe, but the brand expanded over the years to cater for a raft of different sports. American basketball icon George Mikan, who played with the Minneapolis Lakers in the 40s and 50s, wore this model. Baseball star Johnny Bench and boxer Sugar Ray Leonard raised the brand's profile further in the 1960s and 1970s. By the late 70s, PRO-Keds had become *the* brand to wear in New York, influenced heavily by hip-hop.

Later, with heightened competition, the brand seemed to fall into obscurity. PRO-Keds closed down in 1986, only to reappear in 2002 when several classic models were reissued in an attempt to capitalize on the brand's rich heritage.

PRO-KEDS **ROYAL**

THIS WAS THE ORIGINAL B-BOY CHOICE.

The PRO-Keds
Royal was launched in
1949. In the early 1970s,
it proved a real hit with streetwise kids
in the neighbourhoods of New York, and
before long it had gained cult status.

The canvas upper of the Royal offered
comfort and durability, and it was
available in high- and low-top versions.

SHOE DATA

FIRST RELEASED
1949
ORIGINAL PURPOSE
Basketball
EXAMPLES SHOWN
Stüssy editions
NOTES
PRO-Keds closed down
in 1986, but it was
relaunched in 2002. ▪

PRO-KEDS
ROYAL PLUS

THE SIGNATURE RED AND NAVY STRIPES BECAME INSTANTLY RECOGNIZABLE.

The PRO-Keds Royal Plus was available in a high- and low-top version. It soon became the favourite footwear of some of the biggest names on and off the basketball court.

177

ROYAL PLUS

SHOE DATA

FIRST RELEASED
1971
ORIGINAL PURPOSE
Basketball
EXAMPLE SHOWN
Reissue
NOTES
Nate Archibald, who played for the Kansas City Kings, wore the Royal Plus. ■

PRO-KEDS
SHOTMAKER

A STYLISH PERFORMANCE BASKETBALL SHOE

SHOTMAKER

With a herringbone outsole design, the PRO-Keds
Shotmaker came in a high or a low top. Numerous
colourways were produced, mainly on white
leather. In 2003, PRO-Keds reissued the
Shotmaker in different coloured leathers,
including red, blue and black. The reissues
featured the thicker stripe and arrow that
PRO-Keds started to use from the early
1980s onwards.

SHOE DATA

FIRST PRODUCED
1970s
ORIGINAL PURPOSE
Basketball
EXAMPLES SHOWN
Reissues
NOTES
Basketball star
Ralph Sampson
wore the Shotmaker
in the early 1980s.

PUMA

Puma is one of the best-known sports brands in the world, and the company's history is as exciting and varied as its range of shoes. The brand's roots are shared with adidas and go back to 1924 when a new footwear company called Gebrüder-Dassler Schuhfabrik was founded in Herzogenaurach, Germany. It wasn't until 1948 that the Puma name was first used with the formation of Puma Schuhfabrik Rudolf Dassler – now known simply as Puma.

Rudolf Dassler started the brand after a bitter feud with his brother Adolph, who went on to produce adidas. The Puma Atom – the brand's first soccer shoe – was launched in that same year. It was not long before celebrated sportsmen wore the brand at key events. For example, in 1952, runner Josef Barthel of Luxembourg brought Puma its first Olympic Gold when he won the 1500 m in Helsinki. The 'formstripe', introduced in 1956, has been the trademark of the brand ever since. Far from being a mere aesthetic addition, the strip gives extra strength and stability to the upper section of each shoe.

The 1960s brought Puma its fair share of drama – particularly 1968, which was an important year for the brand, with the introduction of the modern cat logo, and the Olympic Games in Mexico. An incident involving 200 m champion Tommie Smith, who won in Puma spikes, made the 1968 Games notorious. As he took the stand to receive the gold medal, barefoot with his Pumas beside him, Smith and teammate John Carlos made the black power salute in protest of the inequality still endured by African-Americans at that time. He left his sneakers on the rostrum for all to see, and the Olympic Committee expelled both protesters from the Olympic Village.

Other sporting legends to have been associated with the brand include tennis superstar Boris Becker, who put his name to one of the best-known signature shoes (page 183), and soccer star Diego Maradona. However, Puma's heritage is also interwoven with the b-boy culture and music, and with the arrival of hip-hop and punk the Puma formstripe became an increasingly frequent and prominent sight on the street. Puma was also popular among skateboarders. In fact, skaters were wearing Suedes (pages 186–187) and Baskets (pages 188–189) in the early 1990s, long before Puma even started to develop a shoe for skating.

Puma has always strived to stay at the forefront of technology, and the twentieth century witnessed the development of a number of innovative Puma inventions, including the Disc system in 1991 (a laceless mechanism for adjusting a shoe's fit) and CELL (said to be the first foam-free midsole) in 1996. The Disc has since been integrated in a number of different models. Yet, for all the technological inroads made by Puma over the years, it is the classics that remain the favourites among sneaker enthusiasts the world over.

SHOE DATA

FIRST RELEASED
1999
ORIGINAL PURPOSE
Lifestyle
EXAMPLES SHOWN
Originals
NOTES
The Mostro is one
of Puma's best-selling
shoes ever. ■

MOSTRO

PUMA **MOSTRO**

THE DOUBLE STRAP DESIGN WAS A WHOLE NEW DIRECTION FOR PUMA.

Created with the fashion / lifestyle market in mind, the Mostro looked like an ideal climbing shoe. The spiked outsole and criss-cross Velcro strap were unique.

SHOE DATA

FIRST RELEASED
2001
ORIGINAL PURPOSE
Motorsports – F1
EXAMPLE SHOWN
Original
NOTES
The ideal shoe for the
motorsports enthusiast,
and a lifestyle statement
at the same time. ■

SPEED CAT

PUMA **SPEED CAT**

WITH THE PROFILE OF A SPEEDING BULLET, THE SPEED CAT LIVES UP TO ITS NAME.

The Puma Speed Cat has a similar tip to the Mostro. Although designed for motorsports, the Speed Cat became extremely popular during the early 2000s as a casual / fashion shoe and is produced in an array of colourways and fabrics. One really attractive feature of this model is the Puma cat, which sits proudly on the toe-guard of the shoe.

ORIGINAL ->

183

BECKER

PUMA **BECKER**

A BOLD SHOE
FOR A CLASS ACT

Boris Becker ensured his place among the all-time tennis greats by
becoming the youngest player to win the men's singles at Wimbledon.
He was just seventeen. Puma managed to capture this achievement in the
Becker, one of the best-known signature tennis shoes, by using a simple but
striking design. His signature was added later.

   The soft nappa leather upper was comfortable and durable, whilst
the sole featured an exposed EVA wedge for stability and manoeuvrability.
The terry collar lining inside the shoe absorbed any moisture but kept the
foot cool.

SHOE DATA

FIRST PRODUCED
1980s
ORIGINAL PURPOSE
Tennis
EXAMPLES SHOWN
Original / Reissue
NOTES
Puma also released the
Boris Becker Ace model.

SHOE DATA

FIRST RELEASED
1983
ORIGINAL PURPOSE
Tennis
EXAMPLE SHOWN
Reissue
NOTES
This model was endorsed
by Argentinian tennis
legend Guillermo Vilas. ■

G. VILAS

184

THE THRILLS EDITION

SHOE DATA

FIRST RELEASED
1983
ORIGINAL PURPOSE
Training
EXAMPLES SHOWN
Reissue / Thrills edition
NOTES
This 1980s sneaker
enjoyed a mid-1990s
revival. ■

CALIFORNIA

PUMA **CALIFORNIA**

ONE OF THE MOST STRIKING CASUAL TRAINING SHOES IN THE RANGE

The distinctive styling of the California – with its low-slung design – has won a place in sneaker history. However, there is a lot more to this shoe than first meets the eye.

The main body of the upper was constructed from nylon with the nubuck Puma vamp (the large stripe) on the side panel. Its PU sole was invincible and impossible to wear down.

The external arch support accommodated every possible angle of the foot's movement, while the moulded footbed was anatomically formed to ensure comfort.

PUMA G. VILAS

THE CALIFORNIA'S LEATHER COUSIN

Its ultra thick outsole gave G. Vilas an edge and tennis players extra cushioning. The upper let the foot breathe, even during extensive exercise, while the perforated vamp added ventilation holes to the side panels without affecting the durability of the upper. Along with earlier Puma models such as the California, the G. Vilas became synonymous with the soccer casuals scene.

185

PUMA TRIMM QUICK / TRIMM FIT

IT'S A FAMILY AFFAIR.

This family comprises the Trimm Quick, the Trimm Fit and the S. P. A. Trimm. The Fit, with its Velcro lacing system, took Velcro technology one step further, while the S. P. A. Trimm boasts the revolutionary S. P. A. technology, invented by Puma in 1976.

TRIMM QUICK / FIT

SHOE DATA

FIRST PRODUCED
1970s
ORIGINAL PURPOSE
Training
EXAMPLE SHOWN
Reissue
NOTES
S. P. A. stands for 'Sportabsatz' (sports heel) and claims to reduce the risk of injury by 30%. ■

186

THE BUJU BANTON EDITION

PUMA
SUEDE-STATE-CLYDE

THE ARCHETYPAL PUMA MODEL, THIS SNEAKER IS
A WORLDWIDE CLASSIC THAT HAS STOOD THE TEST
OF TIME – AND PASSED.

Also known as Puma States (or Puma Clydes in the case of the signature version), the Suede has become one of the best-loved sneakers. A basic design with clean styling was counterbalanced by a whole series of colours. Along with the adidas Superstar, the Suede was the staple of every b-boy's daily outfit. On the street, a pair of Suedes had to look totally fresh and clean and were worn with contrasting hats, tube socks, tracksuits, denim and goose-down puffa jackets. Finding the most original colourway and matching the laces became a popular pastime, and making the shoes look wide with fat laces and folded socks under the tongue was a must.

In the 1990s, with the old-skool revival, true connoisseurs – having kept their shoes from the 1980s – were pleased to see a whole new selection of colours come on to the market as fresh interest pushed Suedes to the forefront of fashion once again. Along with the adidas Gazelle, the acid-jazz music scene also embraced the shoe as it reflected the retro feel at the time and looked really good with cord trousers, although it is such a versatile shoe that it can be worn with almost anything. The revamped versions included a hemp edition, which became popular with skaters. It was cheap, widely available and robust.

SUEDE-STATE-CLYDE

SHOE DATA

FIRST RELEASED
1968
ORIGINAL PURPOSE
Basketball
EXAMPLES SHOWN
Reissues
NOTES
The Puma Clyde was inspired by basketball ace Walter Frazier.

↑
EVISU EDITION

PUMA **BASKET**

THE LEATHER VERSION
OF THE SUEDE, KNOWN
AS THE BASKET, IS ANOTHER
CLASSIC IN THE PUMA
ARSENAL.

Although almost identical to the Suede, the Basket had its own
identity due to its many variations. The Puma stripe was often found
on a perforated version of the Basket, and there were high tops as well
as the standard low-top edition. While white was the most common colour,
others featured red leather with a white stripe, and black with a white stripe.

The Basket proved a popular winter option for Puma Suede fans. Although
more durable than its suede counterpart, it was slightly heavier and less
flexible. In 1995, Puma released the Super Basket to celebrate the
company's longevity. This version featured a much thicker outsole.

SHOE DATA

BASKET

FIRST RELEASED
1968
ORIGINAL PURPOSE
Basketball
EXAMPLES SHOWN
Reissues / Evisu
NOTES
Appearing in the hip-
hop film *Beat Street*
transformed this model
from the shoe from the
block to a worldwide,
classic b-boy icon. ■

SHOE DATA

FIRST RELEASED
1986
ORIGINAL PURPOSE
Basketball
EXAMPLES SHOWN
Originals
NOTES
The Sky II also came in
a low skate edition.

PUMA
SKY II

AN ICONIC BASKETBALL SHOE

This basketball shoe was designed for the
serious player, but that didn't stop it becoming
one of the most stylish shoes in the range.
The wedge / outsole used an injection process
to add durability to the rubber compound,
but it remained lightweight. The Velcro strap
and lacing system made the shoe a perfect fit.
It came in some great colourways, but the Boston
Celtics and the LA Lakers editions are among the
most sought-after.

SKY II LOW SKATE EDITION

PUMA
SLIPSTREAM / THE BEAST

THE SLIPSTREAM WAS A PUMA BASKETBALL CLASSIC. THE BEAST WAS ITS ALTER EGO.

The Slipstream, a basic basketball model from the 1980s, featured all the latest technological developments and was available in high- and low-top versions. Puma also brought out a more daring offshoot in the 1980s known as the Beast. When the Beast was first reissued in Japan in 2002, it featured fake animal skin / fur on the upper. The idea of adding fake skin or fur has since been taken up by a string of different brands.

SHOE DATA

FIRST PRODUCED
1980s
ORIGINAL PURPOSE
Basketball
EXAMPLES SHOWN
Reissues
NOTES
Puma also released the Slipstream in a low-top version. ◼

PUMA TX - 3

A COMPACT FEAT OF DESIGN

Designed for superior stability, motion control and maximum shock absorption, the TX - 3 looked like a serious item of running kit. Whilst the lower half of this model was equipped with advanced features such as the tri-density removable innersole, the upper kept the vibe running throughout the entire shoe.

The unique combination of pig skin and mesh also boasted reflective details for heightened visibility. A true performance shoe, the TX - 3 took Puma's technology to a new level.

192

TX - 3

SHOE DATA

FIRST RELEASED
1985
ORIGINAL PURPOSE
Running
EXAMPLES SHOWN
Reissues
NOTES
The TX - 3 was reissued in 2004 in multiple colourways.

PUMA RS1

THE SCALED-DOWN VERSION OF THE RS-COMPUTER

In 1985, Puma developed its answer to the adidas Micro Pacer in the form of the RS-Computer. With its integrated computer, this model could electronically record and calculate anything that a runner wanted to know about his or her athletic performance.

The RS1 was basically the same shoe, but without the computer. A clean design and streamlined style to the upper was rounded off with a high-quality running sole. Timeless styling has enabled this shoe to maintain its popularity over the years.

193

RS1

SHOE DATA

FIRST RELEASED
1985
ORIGINAL PURPOSE
Running
EXAMPLES SHOWN
Reissues
NOTES
Featuring the Multiplex IV wedge system for shock absorption and stability, it was reissued in 2004.

PUMA ROMA

GERMAN ENGINEERING WITH A TOUCH OF ITALIAN CHIC

Puma's Roma was brought out in 1968. Its upper was made of split cowhide, and the padded tongue and reinforced heel provided extra comfort. The inside of the shoe boasted an orthopaedic arch support. During the 1980s, this model became a firm favourite among the soccer casuals.

SHOE DATA

FIRST RELEASED
1968
ORIGINAL PURPOSE
Training
EXAMPLES SHOWN
Reissues / Lazio edition
NOTES
The Roma was released in 2003 in a colourway dedicated to the Italian soccer team Lazio.

ROMA

PUMA TAHARA

THE IDEAL INDOOR TRAINING SHOE

Produced in the 1970s, this shoe featured a distinctive gum sole and a nylon / suede combination upper. It was popular with soccer casuals during the 1980s and helped cheer many teams to victory all over Europe.

SHOE DATA

FIRST PRODUCED
1970s
ORIGINAL PURPOSE
Training
EXAMPLE SHOWN
Original
NOTES
The Tahara was reissued in the early 2000s. ▪

PUMA DALLAS

THE STATE WAS NOT THE ONLY SHOE TO WEAR ITS SUEDE WITH PRIDE.

The Dallas was a basketball classic. For Europe's b-boy community, the Dallas was second only to the Suede and the State. All in all, this was a fantastic sneaker!

SHOE DATA

FIRST PRODUCED
1980s
ORIGINAL PURPOSE
Basketball
EXAMPLE SHOWN
Original
NOTES
Another version of the Dallas featured a darker blue / sky-blue colourway. It also had a different shaped toe box to the model shown. ▪

PUMA RALPH SAMPSON

THE PERFECT MIX OF KNOWLEDGE, TECHNOLOGY AND EXPERIENCE

This basketball shoe was made famous by the legendary pro Ralph Sampson, who played for the Houston Rockets, and whose size seventeen feet became a symbol of the game. When he began working with Puma's design technicians to create this model, he was able to mix his experience of playing on the court with their knowledge of shoe technology. The result was a basketball shoe with cutting-edge components, support and durability.

196

RALPH SAMPSON

SHOE DATA

FIRST RELEASED
1980
ORIGINAL PURPOSE
Basketball
EXAMPLE SHOWN
Original low-top version
NOTES
Ralph Sampson was National Player of the Year three times. ▪

DISC HIGH

197

PUMA DISC

A TESTAMENT TO PUMA'S TECHNOLOGICAL EXPERTISE

The adjustable disc on the top of the Puma Disc eliminated the need for laces. In practice, it looked very similar to Reebok's Pump system but it used completely different technology.

The ability to fine-tune the fit of a shoe was a major breakthrough, and word spread quickly through the athletic community. The outsole featured DuPont's Hypalon rubber for maximum cushioning and impact absorption, while the upper was made from a combination of mesh and Aeroprene for flexibility.

DISC

SHOE DATA

FIRST RELEASED
1994
ORIGINAL PURPOSE
Running
EXAMPLES SHOWN
Reissues
NOTES
There were two other similar models in the Disc range: the Disc System Terrain and the Disc System Lady Blaze.

SPRINT

SHOE DATA

FIRST RELEASED
1970
ORIGINAL PURPOSE
Cycling
EXAMPLE SHOWN
Reissue
NOTES
The Sprint was reissued
in 2000. ▪

EASY RIDER

SHOE DATA

FIRST RELEASED
1982
ORIGINAL PURPOSE
Running
EXAMPLES SHOWN
Reissues
NOTES
Puma also released the
Easy Rider in a high-top
camouflage edition. ▪

PUMA EASY RIDER
A CLASSIC JOGGER THAT PACKS
A POWERFUL PUNCH

Viewed as revolutionary on its release, the Easy Rider combined a nylon and suede upper with a carbonized multi-level sole to produce a stable and comfortable shoe. It has since become one of the most popular shoes in the Puma line-up.

The use of technological features, such as the PU wedge system and Federbein outsole design, gave it 'breakthrough' status. It subsequently became the starting point for several other Puma models.

CAMO EDITION

PUMA 500M

RUNNING WITH A NEW NAME

First released in 1980, the Cross Country (as the 500M was then known) was developed by Puma France specifically for cross-country running and originally featured spikes on the outsole. In those days it was known for its distinctive long tongue, which was designed to protect the foot from stones and other rubble that cross-country courses can throw up. The new running shoe version has been renamed the 500M.

500M

SHOE DATA

FIRST RELEASED
1980
ORIGINAL PURPOSE
Running
EXAMPLE SHOWN
Reissue
NOTES
The 500M was originally called the Cross Country.

PUMA SPRINT
THE LOW-PROFILE NARROW SILHOUETTE OF THIS SNEAKER WAS INSPIRED BY A VINTAGE 1970S CYCLING SHOE.

On its launch in 1970, the Sprint became one of Puma's best-selling models. Today, it remains as popular as it was then and is worn by kids across Europe.

The form-fitting nature of the Sprint makes it extremely comfortable, but it also has an edgy, modern look to it. Its stylish appeal is cemented by a medial side hook and loop closure, and a soft upper.

200

SHOE DATA

FIRST RELEASED
1971
ORIGINAL PURPOSE
Training
EXAMPLE SHOWN
Original
NOTES
When Pelé played, he would always wait until he came through the tunnel before tying his laces.

PUMA PELÉ BRAZIL

A SHOE DESIGNED TO CELEBRATE A TRUE SPORTING ICON

One of the most talked-about endorsement models, this shoe completely rocked the boat when it was released in the early 1970s. Pelé was arguably the greatest soccer player of his era and the top Brazilian goal scorer of all time. His signature kicked off a whole range of shoes and apparel for Puma.

This shoe came in the vibrant Brazilian colours, but when stripped down to the basics it looked like a cross between a Puma Suede and a Puma Dallas with an amended sole. The tread rose around the edge of the sole, giving extra grip. The Pelé Brazil's lightweight appearance was deceptive, however: the sturdiness of the shoe actually meant that it was heavier than the average.

PUMA
ART OF PUMA

A LESSON IN MODERN ART

If you thought that squiggly drawings on shoes were a craze from the 2000s, you were wrong! Featuring the 'Made in West Germany' stamp on the tongue, this sneaker's outrageous design went down a treat in Japan, and it is still sought-after by collectors around the globe.

ART OF PUMA

SHOE DATA

FIRST PRODUCED
1980s
ORIGINAL PURPOSE
Lifestyle
EXAMPLE SHOWN
Original
NOTES
The Art of Puma came in five different versions, each with a different design / print. ■

REEBOK

The Reebok empire originated in the UK. It was founded for one basic reason: people wanted to run faster. In the 1890s, Joseph William Foster was among the first to make spiked running shoes. By 1895, he was making shoes by hand for top runners in his local area. The company, J. W. Foster and Sons, gradually built up an international list of clients.

In 1958, two of the founder's grandsons started a sister company that came to be known as Reebok, named after an African gazelle. However, the turning point came in 1979 when Paul Fireman, a partner in an outdoor sporting goods distributorship, came across Reebok products at an international trade show. Three years later, Fireman purchased the Reebok licence and introduced the brand to the American market. By 1981, Reebok's sales exceeded $1.5 million.

In 1982, Reebok introduced the first athletic shoe designed especially for women: the Freestyle (page 209). The Freestyle remains one of the best-selling styles in Reebok's history. Reebok anticipated and encouraged three major trends that transformed the athletic footwear industry: the aerobic exercise movement, the increasing number of women into sports and exercise, and the acceptance of well-designed athletic footwear by adults for street and casual wear. In the late 1980s, a particularly fertile period began with the Pump technology and continues today with breakthrough technologies like Hexalite and DMX for all fitness activities.

In the late 1990s, Reebok made a strategic move to align its brand with a select few of the world's most talented, exciting athletes. For several years now, the company has focused on those athletes who represent the top level of sports and fitness, including basketball star Allen Iverson and tennis champion Venus Williams.

In 1992, Reebok stamped its presence in the international arena by introducing new shoe styles and performance apparel for individual contestants. Four years later, more than thirty per cent of contestants taking part in the Atlanta Olympic Games were wearing footwear and apparel with the Reebok trademark. Athletes were not the only stars in Reebok's eyes. In 2003, Reebok made history by signing rap superstar Jay-Z, aka Shaun Carter, to create the S. Carter range (page 227).

REEBOK WORKOUT

REEBOK'S FIRST MOVE INTO THE MEN'S FITNESS MARKET

WORKOUT

SHOE DATA

FIRST RELEASED
1986
ORIGINAL PURPOSE
Fitness
EXAMPLES SHOWN
Reissues
NOTES
A popular style was
to lace up the shoe
missing out the
H-strap holes. ■

The Reebok Workout has always been a popular shoe. This is down to its perfect formula: inexpensive and comfortable, it comes in a variety of colourways. The Workout, which has been in production constantly since 1986, was designed as a multi-sports fitness shoe. It is suitable for weight training, light jogging and exercise workouts.

Over the years, Reebok has experimented with its appearance. The outsole has been fashioned in a variety of colours and moulded in a range of shapes. The upper went through a number of design changes too with the use of camouflage and full mesh. The H-strap has also had a splash of colour in the past. The Reebok Workout is a true classic.

REEBOK WORKOUT PLUS

A MORE REFINED VERSION OF THE WORKOUT

First made in the early 1990s, the Reebok Workout Plus has been manufactured under the Reebok Classic umbrella ever since. It always comes in monotone colourways, although Reebok jazzed it up from time to time. The sneaker's white colouring with blue detail, and its combination of a rather aggressive stance and clean lines, are a winning formula.

The use of 3M-style reflective strips on the H-strap was a successful addition. The Classic range has found particular favour among British youths.

WORKOUT PLUS

SHOE DATA

FIRST PRODUCED
1990s
ORIGINAL PURPOSE
Fitness
EXAMPLE SHOWN
Reissue
NOTES
The US and Asia received more colourways of the Reebok Workout Plus than their European counterparts.

REEBOK EX-O-FIT

THE MEN'S VERSION OF THE WOMEN'S REEBOK FREESTYLE

EX-O-FIT

SHOE DATA

FIRST RELEASED
1987
ORIGINAL PURPOSE
Fitness
EXAMPLE SHOWN
Reissue
NOTES
Reebok USA released
an array of colourways
of the Ex-O-Fit in
the 1980s. ▪

The Reebok Ex-O-Fit was designed for the fitness market but became a regular on market stalls. It was simple in design with clean lines.

The low-top version looks strikingly similar to the women's Reebok Freestyle. The high-top edition, on the other hand, looks and feels more like the high-top Workout Plus. The upper was made of soft garment leather, and the high-top model featured a thick ankle strap.

The Ex-O-Fit had minimal branding: the Reebok patch on the side panel and on the heel were the only clues to the identity of the manufacturer. The Ex-O-Fit was reissued in 2000 but only in the basic black and white colourways.

REEBOK CXT

REEBOK'S ATTEMPT AT A MULTIPURPOSE FITNESS SHOE

CXT

SHOE DATA

FIRST PRODUCED
1990s
ORIGINAL PURPOSE
Cross-training
EXAMPLE SHOWN
Original
NOTES
The first CXT featured the
Energy Return System
cushioning technology. ■

The CXT was built for various sports, from tennis to weightlifting. It boasted
Pump technology for a custom fit, and the Hexalite in the midsole had
superior cushioning. The midcut supported the ankle in outdoor sports
like basketball and tennis. The CXT was released in a variety of colourways,
all based on white leather, but it has yet to be reissued.

↑
COW PRINT EDITION

REEBOK FREESTYLE

THE ORIGINAL
AEROBICS SHOE

The Freestyle came in a high- and low-top
version and a variety of colourways. It was
a huge success in the fitness field. Reebok
produced a similar-looking shoe called the
Princess, but it was unable to compete with
the Freestyle.

FREESTYLE

SHOE DATA

FIRST RELEASED
1985
ORIGINAL PURPOSE
Aerobics
EXAMPLES SHOWN
Originals / Cow Print
NOTES
The Freestyle is one
of Reebok's best-selling
shoes of all time.

REEBOK SUPERCOURT

WITH A SLEEK WEDGE PROFILE, THIS SHOE WAS A SPEED DEMON.

Looking every inch a design classic, the Supercourt combined comfort and style. The soft leather upper offered support, while the sexy gum rubber outsole provided traction and durability.

This model was reissued in a multitude of classic colourways including browns, navys and sand, using materials such as nylon, suede and leather. It features a die-cut EVA sockliner for extra cushioning and comfort.

SUPERCOURT

SHOE DATA

FIRST PRODUCED
1980s
ORIGINAL PURPOSE
Running
EXAMPLES SHOWN
Reissues
NOTES
In 2004, Reebok released a camouflage colourway of the Supercourt.

SHOE DATA

FIRST RELEASED
1989
ORIGINAL PURPOSE
Tennis
EXAMPLE SHOWN
Reissue
NOTES
The Reebok Newport
Classic was reissued
in 2000. ▨

REEBOK
NEWPORT CLASSIC

THEY MADE YOU FEEL
LIKE A CHAMP ON
THE TENNIS COURT.

The Newport Classic was a hit with Reebok
collectors and proved particularly popular in
the summer. This was down to its clean lines
and soft leather.

Two colourways of the Newport Classic were
released: an all-white edition and the popular
cream version. The nubbed outsole was the only
aspect of the shoe to give away its true purpose.
In fact, most people thought that the Newport
Classic was for fitness rather than tennis.

REEBOK
CLASSIC NYLON

THE NYLON VERSION OF THE
CLASSIC – AS SIMPLE AS THAT!

The Classic Nylon's upper was made of
breathable nylon mesh with suede trim.
Its sculptured EVA midsole provided extra
lightweight cushioning.

It wasn't an elaborate shoe: it was aimed
at the customer who wanted something simple
and plain, a notion that was reflected in the
Classic Nylon's price. The colourways were
equally straightforward: navy / platinum,
white / grey, and black / white.

CLASSIC NYLON

SHOE DATA

FIRST RELEASED
1987
ORIGINAL PURPOSE
Running
EXAMPLE SHOWN
Reissue
NOTES
In 2004, the Classic
was given new and
refreshing colourways. ■

REEBOK CLASSIC

UBIQUITOUS AND NOTORIOUS

The Classic leather edition was designed for the casual consumer: it was clean, simple and easy to wear. With bright colours and wild technology banned, this was the gentleman's sneaker!

Over the years, Reebok released more colourways, including monotones in green, navy, white, red and black. It's not only the colours that have changed since its launch. There have been slip-ons, mules and high-top editions, both with and without straps.

In 2003, a City edition was created. This featured graffiti-style illustrations on its see-through outsole. Once called the 'Pub Shoe' in the UK, the Classic has also been associated with some rather shady characters. Needless to say, this notoriety has given it more street cred than most.

CLASSIC

SHOE DATA

FIRST RELEASED
1987
ORIGINAL PURPOSE
Running / Casual
EXAMPLES SHOWN
Reissues
NOTES
The Classic is one of Reebok's all-time bestsellers, especially in the UK. ▪

214

216

REEBOK HXL

ONE FOR EVERY REEBOK ENTHUSIAST'S COLLECTION

The Reebok HXL was the only Reebok running shoe at the time to offer a custom fit through two pump chambers positioned strategically in the arch and ankle collar. The midsole featured Hexalite cushioning technology encapsulated in the heel, which was visible through the bottom of the outsole.

The air was pumped into the air chambers by pressing the large red rubber button on the sides of the shoe. This would provide a snug fit, and it was so effective that the laces became secondary. Air could be released by holding down the small button. Another excellent feature was the translucent straps.

HXL

SHOE DATA

FIRST RELEASED
1993
ORIGINAL PURPOSE
Running
EXAMPLE SHOWN
Reissue
NOTES
This was the first running shoe to incorporate Reebok's Pump technology.

REEBOK
COURT VICTORY

WHO CARES ABOUT 'PUMP'
WHEN YOU'VE GOT A SHOE
THAT LOOKS THIS GOOD!

The Court Victory featured Reebok's Pump technology. It boasted inflatable air chambers inside the tongue and the internal ankle support, which together ensured a custom fit.

However, the Pump wasn't its only exciting feature. It also included Hexalite technology in the heel.

The tennis-ball green used on the shoe was a nice touch. The Court Victory was reissued in 2003.

COURT VICTORY

SHOE DATA

FIRST RELEASED
1989
ORIGINAL PURPOSE
Tennis
EXAMPLE SHOWN
Reissue
NOTES
Michael Chang wore
the Court Victory. ▪

220

REEBOK INSTA PUMP FURY

INSTA PUMP FURY

SHOE DATA

FIRST RELEASED
1993
ORIGINAL PURPOSE
Running
EXAMPLES SHOWN
Reissues
NOTES
One of the lightest models
in the Reebok range,
it combines performance
with stylish design. ◼

AT THE CUTTING EDGE OF DESIGN

The Insta Pump Fury was the main shoe in Reebok's Pump range. This shoe was the first model to utilize full-length pump technology: the lacing system was dispensed with altogether, as the inflated front panel held the foot firmly and securely in place. The shoe was an instant success with Japanese collectors, and pump fever soon made its way to Europe, where consumers liked to coordinate the shoe with their wardrobe.

It was relaunched in 1996 as the Pump Fury – dropping the 'Insta' from the name. Many of the problems associated with the 1993 original were addressed in this new edition. The addition of Hexalite to the sole made the front section stronger and more rigid.

The shoe has been modernized with a variety of colourways. There have also been several collaborations between Reebok and other enterprises. One such collaborative project resulted in the launch of a Chanel version.

REEBOK PRO LEGACY

JUST AS BASKETBALL WAS TAKING THE WORLD BY STORM, THE PRO LEGACY HIT THE MARKET.

Back in the 1980s, when the NBA's greatest stars were making a name for themselves, Reebok wanted to put its own stamp on the basketball market, which at the time was dominated by Nike and Converse. The company approached two stars of the NBA Champions and the Boston Celtics: Danny Ainge and Dennis Johnson, who had sponsorship deals with Nike. They signed with Reebok in 1986, and the rest is history.

The Pro Legacy was worn by both Ainge and Johnson, and was available in high- and low-top versions and a variety of colourways. The white / black / gold and white / green / black were the most sought-after, however. Reebok reissued the Pro Legacy in 2003 in the original colourways.

SHOE DATA

FIRST PRODUCED
1980s
ORIGINAL PURPOSE
Basketball
EXAMPLES SHOWN
Reissues
NOTES
Special Argyle skateboarding editions were produced in 2003.

PRO LEGACY

REEBOK PUMP OMNI

SIMPLE BUT VERY EFFECTIVE

The Reebok Pump Omni had a starring role in the 1991 All Star Dunk contest. The competition winner was Dee Brown of the Boston Celtics, who was wearing the Pump Omni Lite.

The Pump chambers in the ankle collar offered the ultimate in comfort and fit technology, but it wasn't the shoe's only innovation. The Pump Omni Lite boasted Hexalite technology, which could be seen through the visible window in the bottom of the outsole.

The Pump Omni Lite was reissued in 2002, and Reebok produced a variety of new colourways in 2003, including basketball team colourways. In 2004, Reebok JPSE released a special outdoor edition using completely different materials – nubuck and suede.

PUMP OMNI

SHOE DATA

FIRST RELEASED
1991
ORIGINAL PURPOSE
Basketball
EXAMPLES SHOWN
Reissues
NOTES
Reebok produced an Omni Lite SE edition, which had mesh side panels instead of leather. ▪

REEBOK
COMMITMENT

AN AUTHORITY ON COURT

COMMITMENT

SHOE DATA

FIRST RELEASED
1989
ORIGINAL PURPOSE
Basketball
EXAMPLE SHOWN
Reissue
NOTES
The Reebok Commitment
was worn by the Boston
Celtic players in the
late 1980s.

The Reebok Commitment packed
a powerful punch on the basketball
courts. It was produced in high- and low-
top versions, and the Reebok lettering on
the side panel was huge. The forefoot strap
was used to keep the foot secure, and the outsole
had a flared section added for stability.

Reebok released numerous colourways of the
Commitment, but the best has to be the classic
black / white high top. This model made a
reappearance in 2003 in that same colourway.

REEBOK ALIEN STOMPER

ALIENS DIDN'T STAND A CHANCE AGAINST THIS SHOE.

The Alien Stomper was originally produced for director James Cameron's 1986 sci-fi blockbuster *Aliens*. Leading lady Sigourney Weaver wore them in her role as no-nonsense lieutenant Ellen Ripley.

Reebok brought this model down to Earth a year later, but finding a pair often turned into mission in itself as they were not widely available. The laceless upper oozed futuristic style; the ribbed tongue and double straps paid tribute to their astronautical inspiration.

The purpose of the shoe has always remained something of a mystery. It was reissued in Japan in 2003.

ALIEN STOMPER

SHOE DATA

FIRST RELEASED
1987
ORIGINAL PURPOSE
Space travel
EXAMPLES SHOWN
Originals
NOTES
Reebok released a special collaborative model with the Atmos store in Japan in 2004. ◼

225

REEBOK AMAZE

A SHOE WITH WOW FACTOR

The Reebok Amaze was produced at the tail end of the 1980s, released in a high and a low top. The high-top version featured an ankle strap and was reissued in 2002 in a multitude of colourways. Reebok also introduced the so-called International series, which was produced in limited quantities.

The soft, leather upper provided comfort and support, while a moulded sockliner and full cup wall gave extra cushioning. The design of the rubber outsole ensured traction and durability.

SHOE DATA

FIRST PRODUCED
1980s
ORIGINAL PURPOSE
Basketball
EXAMPLE SHOWN
Reissue
NOTES
In 2004, Reebok introduced a limited edition Puerto Rican model. ■

AMAZE

REEBOK S. CARTER

HISTORY IN THE MAKING

When Reebok released the S. Carter in 2003, it was the first time that the company had signed up an entertainer. The collection – a fusion of sports and celebrity – was a collaboration between the hip-hop rap star Jay-Z (aka Shaun Carter) and Reebok's team of talented Rbk (Reebok's label) designers.

The first editions of the S. Carter were made of soft leather, with coloured detailing, and were produced in various colourways. Its design bears certain similarities to 1980s Gucci footwear. In 2004, Reebok produced a brown / beige canvas edition. A mid-top version was also released later that year.

REEBOK G UNIT G-6

SO POPULAR THAT THE ORIGINAL PRODUCTION RUN SOLD OUT IN DAYS

The G Unit G-6 was launched in 2003. It was the first model in a collection by Rbk called G Unit, the result of a collaboration between Reebok and hip-hop superstars G Unit.

The styling was quite subtle: the only indication that it was a collaborative project was the lettering on the side panel and the tongue. A second version of the G-6 – the G-6 Ice – featured a see-through outsole.

VANS

Paul Van Doren founded the Vans shoe company after learning how to make sneakers on America's East Coast. The idea behind the brand was to sell directly to the consumer, cutting out the retail buyers in the process and therefore offering a cheaper product. In 1966, Paul moved the company out to California with his partners Jim Van Doren, Gordy Lee and Serge D'Elia and built the Vans factory. The first Vans store was opened, offering three different styles of shoe.

Towards the mid-1970s, skateboarding had become a major pastime, and Vans was firmly established as the shoe of choice for most skaters. Skaters began to give the company feedback on its products, often requesting new colours and combinations. As a result, Vans created a skater-designed shoe: the ERA. The input from two of the leading professional skaters – Stacy Peralta and Tony Alva – proved that the company was willing to listen to skaters' needs.

In the 1980s, Vans branched out with shoes for other sports, such as baseball and basketball. However, as the company ploughed more and more of its profits into the new ranges, it ended up having to sell the new styles for less than they were costing to make. This had disastrous results, and Vans had to file for bankruptcy.

The company was restructured, and in 1988 the owners sold it to the McCown De Leeuw Company, giving the brand a new lease of life. Manufacture moved from the US to Asia in the mid-1990s, as the traditional vulcanization techniques Vans had pioneered were becoming less cost-efficient.

The Vans Half Cab model (page 231), named after legendary pro skater Steve Caballero, became one of the classic and most recognized skate shoes. Vans Chukkas and various other models became very popular during the 'cut-down shoes' trend in the early 1990s, when skaters would cut off their jeans around the ankles and then take an inch or so off their shoes, which were then sealed with stickers to prevent fraying. This gave the ankle room to move during the small wheel / flip tricks. Today, the brand sponsors some of the world's finest skaters, including Jim Greco, Geoff Rowley, John Cardiel and newcomers Bastien Salabanzi and Flo Marfaing.

VANS **ERA**

INSPIRED BY SKATERS, CREATED BY VANS

SHOE DATA

ERA

FIRST RELEASED
1976
ORIGINAL PURPOSE
Skateboarding
EXAMPLES SHOWN
Reissues
NOTES
Original colours were
two-tone navy / red.
This was followed up
with navy / yellow and
navy / light blue. ◼

Vans was already a firm favourite among skaters when pros Stacy Peralta, Jay Adams and Tony Alva (of the infamous Z-Boys / Dogtown skate crews) helped the company to create the ERA – one of the first shoes specifically designed for skateboarding.

Released in March 1976, it instantly became a bestseller, with demand often outstripping supply. An elaboration on the original 44 model, the ERA featured a padded edge and collar and was the first shoe to carry the Vans 'Off The Wall' logo.

Vans became popular with BMX riders in the 1980s. The sole was sufficiently flexible to feel the tyres during flatland freestyle, but also sturdy enough to survive racing and dirt jumping.

VANS **HALF CAB**

A CLASSIC FOR AN ICON

One of the original signature skate shoes, this model has stood the test
of time, even in the face of extraordinary technological developments.
The soles are thin enough to allow the skater to feel the board beneath
his or her feet, but are extremely hard-wearing. The side protection area
with double stitching keeps the front end tidy.

   The original high-top version became one of the main shoes in the 'cutting
down' era of skateboarding. Vans took this customization on board and
created the Half Cab model, a technically superior version of what skaters
were trying to achieve at that time.

HALF CAB

SHOE DATA

FIRST RELEASED
1985
ORIGINAL PURPOSE
Skateboarding
EXAMPLE SHOWN
Reissue
NOTES
One of the few shoes
to maintain popularity
for over a decade, this
true skating classic
is credited with
resurrecting the
Vans brand.

VANS
SK8 HIGH

A FIRM FAVOURITE WITH SKATEBOARDERS FOR NEARLY THIRTY YEARS

In the design of this model, Vans added a padded collar to address the ankle injuries sustained by skaters. Many kids were hurting themselves in skateparks where their boards would fly off the sides of the ramps.

The classic 'Off The Wall' outsole was durable, but the toe ventilation system stopped the foot from getting too hot and sweaty. The suede side protection on the front section stopped the upper getting ripped, while the canvas side panels kept the shoe flexible.

As well as being an excellent shoe for skating, the Vans SK8 High is also regarded as a classic item from the US hardcore punk and rock kid's wardrobe. Bands like Gang Green, Suicidal Tendencies and Circle Jerks made the SK8 the shoe to have, and Social Distortion also collaborated with Vans on their own version. This is a basic model, but one that doesn't need any alterations.

SK8 HIGH

233

SHOE DATA

FIRST PRODUCED
1970s
ORIGINAL PURPOSE
Skateboarding
EXAMPLES SHOWN
Reissues
NOTES
This shoe has been worn by many of the world's best skaters and, while it doesn't offer the protection and padding of many of today's designs, it still holds up well. ■

234

SHOE DATA

FIRST RELEASED
1973
ORIGINAL PURPOSE
Skateboarding
EXAMPLES SHOWN
Reissues
NOTES
Back in the good old
days, Vans would make
bespoke Slip-Ons
to meet customers'
specific colour or
fabric requirements. ■

VANS
SLIP-ON

FROM BACKSIDE LIPSLIDES TO BMX FREESTYLE – THIS SHOE HAD THE ATTITUDE RIGHT.

This classic deck / skate shoe with a canvas upper seems to have been around for decades, but it remains the leader in its field. Although skate-shoe technology has moved on considerably over the years, some hardcore old skool skaters still wear the Slip-On.

It's all about attitude! With its countless colour combinations and patterns – chequerboard, flames, palm trees, skulls, flags, and so on – this shoe seems to have the winning formula.

Vans has collaborated with many companies over the years, producing exclusive colourways with brands such as X-Girl, Addict, Taito Corporation, Dogtown, Silas, Beams and even Walt Disney.

TAITO & SPACE INVADERS COLLABORATION

AND NOT FORGETTING...

THE OTHER PLAYERS IN THE SNEAKER FIELD. THEY MIGHT NOT
BE AS LARGE IN STATURE AS THE OTHER BRANDS IN THIS BOOK,
BUT THEY HAVE ALL PLAYED A PART IN THE SHOE INDUSTRY.
SOME, LIKE EWING, ARE NO LONGER AROUND, WHILE OTHERS
ARE THE LIMITED EDITION 'RARE' SHOES LIKE THE A BATHING
APE BAPESTA. WITH THEIR OWN STYLES AND TECHNOLOGIES,
THESE BRANDS HAVE BEEN INCLUDED BECAUSE THEY BROUGHT
SOMETHING UNIQUE TO THE INDUSTRY – WHAT YOU ARE
ABOUT TO SEE ARE SOME GREAT SHOES, SOME OF WHICH
YOU MAY NOT HAVE HEARD OF...

JAZZ

SHOE DATA

FIRST RELEASED
1984
ORIGINAL PURPOSE
Running
EXAMPLES SHOWN
Reissues
NOTES
Leather editions were also
produced: the Jazz LX.
All-suede editions were
brought out in 2003. ■

SAUCONY
JAZZ

A PERFECT COMBINATION OF CLEAN LINES, GREAT COLOURS AND SUEDE

The upper on this classic running shoe was made of nylon and suede. The pattern of the rubber outsole provided superior traction. This was totally original and had never been seen before on any other running shoe.

The Saucony Jazz was released in an assortment of colourways. Atmos, a cult sneaker store in Japan, collaborated with clothing label Swagger and Saucony to produce a special Jazz. This Jazz had an interesting mix of denim and leather and is extremely collectable – it was only released in Japan in small quantities. The Jazz remains Saucony's best-selling shoe to date.

240

SAUCONY
HANGTIME

A CUT ABOVE THE REST

SHOE DATA

HANGTIME

FIRST RELEASED
1987
ORIGINAL PURPOSE
Basketball
EXAMPLES SHOWN
Reissues
NOTES
In the 1960s, Saucony
produced footwear for
NASA astronauts. ▪

↑
LOW EDITION

The Saucony Hangtime was produced by Spot-Bilt, the company's oldest division. This high-performance basketball shoe was brought out in a variety of colourways.

The model was reintroduced in 2000 under the Saucony name. The reissued editions featured exciting new colours and materials such as suede and nubuck.

K-SWISS
CLASSIC

THE CLASSIC'S DISTINCTIVE LOOK – WITH FIVE BANDS AND D-RINGS – WAS UNIQUE AT THE TIME AND GAVE IT A HARDCORE FOLLOWING.

The K-Swiss Classic was first released in 1966 and was one of the earliest tennis shoes to have a one-piece rubber outsole. The reinforced toepiece was another stunning feature.

CLASSIC

SHOE DATA

FIRST RELEASED
1966
ORIGINAL PURPOSE
Tennis
EXAMPLE SHOWN
Reissue
NOTES
The K-Swiss Classic began as an all-white shoe, but it was brought out in a variety colourways over the years.

EWING **REFLECTIVE**

IT CAME IN A VARIETY OF COLOURWAYS, BUT THE ORANGE AND ROYAL
BLUE SUEDE, THE TEAM COLOURS OF THE NEW YORK KNICKS, WAS
PARTICULARLY STYLISH.

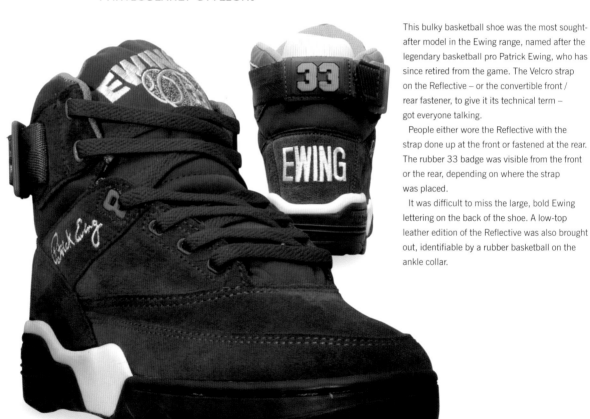

This bulky basketball shoe was the most sought-
after model in the Ewing range, named after the
legendary basketball pro Patrick Ewing, who has
since retired from the game. The Velcro strap
on the Reflective – or the convertible front /
rear fastener, to give it its technical term –
got everyone talking.

People either wore the Reflective with the
strap done up at the front or fastened at the rear.
The rubber 33 badge was visible from the front
or the rear, depending on where the strap
was placed.

It was difficult to miss the large, bold Ewing
lettering on the back of the shoe. A low-top
leather edition of the Reflective was also brought
out, identifiable by a rubber basketball on the
ankle collar.

REFLECTIVE

SHOE DATA

FIRST PRODUCED
1980s
ORIGINAL PURPOSE
Basketball
EXAMPLE SHOWN
Original
NOTES
The '33' on the strap
represents Patrick Ewing's
jersey number. ■

TROOP **PRO MODEL**

FROM RAGS TO RICHES – AND BACK DOWN TO EARTH WITH A BUMP!

The Pro Model remains one of the few sneakers to have enjoyed full rapper endorsement. LL Cool J began wearing the Troop of his own accord. Troop picked up on it and signed him up.

The Pro Model was developed in this environment. It took things to a new level: the fake alligator-skin print, red plastic 'joints', the gold Troop and LL Cool J logos…these were special shoes!

Aside from being among the most extreme high tops on the market, they didn't rely on any specific technological design points. They were strictly for fashion. Needless to say, they didn't last long in the sneaker world. Rumours started to circulate, and the sneaker soon bit the dust.

PRO MODEL

SHOE DATA

FIRST RELEASED
1988
ORIGINAL PURPOSE
Basketball
EXAMPLE SHOWN
Original
NOTES
Troop relaunched this model in 2003, but it failed to make the same impact. ■

DIADORA
BORG ELITE

THE CRÈME DE LA CRÈME

SHOE DATA

FIRST RELEASED
1978
ORIGINAL PURPOSE
Tennis
EXAMPLE SHOWN
Original
NOTES
The shoes came with
a special bag that had
Borg's face on it. ▪

BORG ELITE

Made of kangaroo leather, the Diadora Borg Elite was named after the Swedish tennis pro Bjorn Borg. Recognizing Borg's talent on the court, the Italian brand produced this signature model especially for him. The reissues were quite good, but the originals featured Borg's signature and are far superior. For many soccer casuals, this shoe was the business and stood its ground alongside the likes of the adidas Trimm-Trab.

LACOSTE
TRIBUTE EMB

THIS SHOE HIT THE NAIL ON THE HEAD.

Established in 1933, Lacoste is better known for its crocodile-embroidered polo shirts than its sports shoes, but it really hit the mark with this model. The EMB takes the outsole style to the max!

This is a sneaker for the connoisseur – a gentleman's shoe that still holds respect at street level. With a similar shape to the Reebok Workout and Newport Classic, the Tribute EMB stands out due to its combination of clean lines, subtle branding and that thick gum outsole. Its aggressive stance makes it look like a skate shoe.

245

TRIBUTE EMB

SHOE DATA

FIRST PRODUCED
1980s
ORIGINAL PURPOSE
Training / Lifestyle
EXAMPLE SHOWN
Reissue
NOTES
Another good model from Lacoste is the Reflex.

TRETORN **NYLITE**

A 1980s MUST-HAVE

This shoe was designed and developed in Helsingborg, Sweden. It was manufactured there up until 1977, when the rights of the Tretorn company for the western hemisphere were sold to Colgate-Palmolive. Subsequently, all production moved to the US.

Tretorn's simple sneaker was the first luxury sports shoe to come on to the market. It was a must-have on college campuses throughout the US during the 1980s, and was worn and favoured by presidents and students alike.

NYLITE

SHOE DATA

FIRST RELEASED
1965
ORIGINAL PURPOSE
Tennis
EXAMPLES SHOWN
Reissues
NOTES
This was the shoe that five-time Wimbledon champion Bjorn Borg used in the 1970s in his US games. Chris Evert also won some great victories in this shoe. ▄

GULLWING CLASSIC

This model formed part of the 2001 relaunch of the Nylite. It's a successful blend of a simple, clean style and sheer luxury.

XTL

First released in 1964, the XTL was one of the first leather performance tennis shoes. World-famous American tennis star Billie Jean King ruled the courts in this model during the early 1970s.

TENNY

This model was first produced in around 1936. It was originally sold to the Swedish army as a tennis / leisure shoe for workouts. All recruits were given a pair as part of their basic equipment pack.

A BATHING APE **BAPESTA**

THE COLOURS WILL GET YOU NOTICED.

BAPESTA

Japanese clothing company A Bathing Ape was established in 1993. The Bapesta was inspired by the Nike Air Force 1 and was only available from Footsoldier stores in Asia and Busy Work shops, A Bathing Ape's own chain of retail outlets.

Although this model is almost identical to the Nike Air Force 1, its amazing colourways set it apart and have contributed significantly to its worldwide appeal. The combinations are fantastic. To top it all, it is rumoured that only one hundred pairs of each colourway are actually produced.

SHOE DATA

FIRST RELEASED
2002
ORIGINAL PURPOSE
Lifestyle
EXAMPLES SHOWN
Originals
NOTES
A Bathing Ape also produces another shoe that was influenced by Puma Suede. ▧

1917

CONVERSE ALL STAR

1964

ADIDAS STAN SMITH

1968

PUMA SUEDE

1987

NIKE AIR MAX

1985

NIKE AIR JORDAN

1985

NIKE AIR SOCK RACER

250

1988

TROOP PRO MODEL

1988

ADIDAS ZX 8000

1990

FILA HIKER

2004

ADIDAS ULTRARIDE

2000

NIKE SHOX R4

2000

NIKE AIR PRESTO

1969 →

ADIDAS SUPERSTAR

1971 →

PRO-KEDS ROYAL PLUS

1972

ADIDAS SL 72

ADIDAS MICRO PACER

1984 ←

NIKE WAFFLE RACER

1974 ←

VANS SLIP-ON

1973 ←

1991 →

NIKE AIR 180

1991 →

ADIDAS EQUIPMENT RACING

1991 →

NIKE HUARACHE

NIKE AIR MAX 95

1995 ←

PUMA DISC

1994 ←

REEBOK PUMP FURY

1993 ←

252

COLLECTORS' GUIDE

THERE'S NO SUCH THING AS A TYPICAL COLLECTOR —
IT DIFFERS FROM PERSON TO PERSON. SOME PEOPLE
ENJOY MAINTAINING A COLLECTION OF SHOES THEY
LIKE, WHETHER IT'S BRANDS OR COLOURS THEY'RE GOING
FOR, WHILST OTHERS SIMPLY HAVE SNEAKERS ALONGSIDE
THEIR ADDITIONAL COLLECTIONS, SUCH AS RECORDS
OR ACTION FIGURES.

Some people keep them pristine, unworn and boxed – 'deadstock' is the correct term – whilst others choose to wear all the pairs they buy. Many collectors buy two pairs – one to keep deadstock and one to wear out.

The point is this: it doesn't matter what you do! Good shoes speak for themselves, and it's all in the eye of the beholder. There are, however, some simple tips to follow, which will help you build and care for your collection.

Where to buy

In the past, your average sports store didn't offer the serious sneakerhead much in terms of range, but things have changed since then – being a sneaker fan and collecting sneakers has become an increasingly mainstream concern. If you want reissues or firm favourites that have never gone out of production, a trip to a well-stocked and well-run local sports store will have everything you need, but if you want an original release, or something a bit rarer or more exclusive, you'll have to look beyond these stores – those limited editions and 'rare' collaborations can be found in places like Foot Patrol in London and Alife in New York.

For a really dedicated collector, the most enjoyable way to find sneakers for his or her collection is to take some time to visit thrift stores and flea markets. Often there's nothing much there, but every now and then a real gem can be picked up for a fraction of the price you'd pay elsewhere – the satisfaction of finding something special, having put in some groundwork first, is immeasurable.

The Internet has changed the world of the sneaker collector, both by putting him or her in touch with

each other like never before and by providing more and more places to buy sneakers. The major stores all have good websites, and there is an ever greater number of sneaker trading websites. For those of you who like a good auction, there's always eBay. Details of some of these sources can be found in the resources section on p. 254.

What to buy

Take your time – don't let money burn a hole in your pocket. Instead of buying quickly and without foresight, it's far easier on the wallet to acquire a good collection over a period of time. Give yourself the time to consider the true worth of a re-release, a new design or a deadstock shoe on offer. Don't get caught up in the hype, and avoid gimmicks and poorly detailed re-releases (naming no names, of course). Checking the reviews and forums of sneaker websites is always a good way to see which way the wind is blowing, but beyond that just run with your instincts – if you love a single brand or a single style, then go with it.

Many people make a living buying and selling sneakers that they pick up on their travels and consequently there is a healthy spirit of competition among different collectors. Again, the websites listed on p. 254 are a good way of being introduced to that world.

Hints and tips

Sometimes it can be hard to verify that a sneaker is an original and not a reissue, but there are often clues on the shoes themselves. Old original adidas shoes were made in Europe, with France being particularly popular (although Italy, Austria,

Yugoslavia and Germany also feature). Puma sneakers also have a similar labelling system – their old originals were manufactured in West Germany and Italy. The tongue of an original adidas will tell you where the shoe was made, but watch out for some very convincing reissues – for the adidas Superstar, for instance, where the label on the tongue looks like an original French-manufactured shoe, but under closer scrutiny shows that they were actually made in Vietnam.

Nike shoes have a six-digit code inside the tongue, the last two digits of which give the year of manufacture (95 for 1995, 04 for 2004, etc). The inside of the tongue will also tell you where the shoe was made.

The materials used in some shoes do degrade over time. This doesn't mean that your sneakers are going to turn to dust, but it does mean that for shoes that use PU (polyurethane) in the outsole, particularly from the 70s and early 80s, you should avoid wearing them as the material will crack and crumble with use.

Caring for your collection

Shoe maintenance is important if you're planning on looking after your purchases. There are a few straightforward rules to follow. Storing them in their boxes will keep things organized and in pretty good condition, but you can leave them out if you want to and still keep them in good condition – you don't have to hide them away. However, as is the case with most modern collectables, any shoe is worth more to a collector with its original packaging than without. The box designs used by the brands have often changed over the years and give clues to a shoe's year and place of manufacture, and will prove authenticity of a deadstock shoe – so however you display your collection, don't throw the boxes away. The packaging has become very important (and elaborate) for some shoes (see the Nike Air Pressure on p. 151 and the Onitsuka Tiger Tai Chi on p. 159), so sometimes we're not even dealing with cardboard. Some extreme

253

RESOURCES

THERE ARE MANY PLACES
TO PICK UP SNEAKERS.
SOME PEOPLE LIKE TO
VISIT STORES IN VARIOUS
COUNTRIES, WHILE OTHERS
PREFER TO STAY AT HOME
AND SHOP ONLINE.
THERE ARE ALSO PLENTY
OF WEBSITES WITH
INFORMATION ON
DIFFERENT BRANDS AND
MODELS, MANY WITH FORUMS
THROUGH WHICH YOU CAN
VOICE YOUR OPINION.
WHATEVER YOUR CHOICES,
HERE ARE A FEW PLACES
TO BEGIN YOUR HUNTING...

sneakerheads claim to keep their collection in a fridge – you don't have to take it that far, but whatever turns you on…

Another important tip: if you want to maintain the value of your collection, you need to keep the shoes authentic. In other words, the original laces, packaging (including the tissue paper and promotional material that came in the box) and removable items such as the innersole (or sockliner) mustn't be lost or changed. Such examples can seriously devalue the shoe.

People often ask how sneakers can be cleaned. Simple things like handwashing them with soap and warm water, and using a toothbrush and stain remover to get the marks off the stitching, always help. Particularly with leather shoes, like the adidas Superstar (see pages 28–29), they can look as good as new after cleaning them that way. The washing machine is useful for getting laces back to their original state, and if you put them in a delicates bag (like you use for washing lingerie and stockings) you avoid the risk of them getting caught up in the holes on the washing machine drum. You can also put *certain* shoes through the washing machine (but please check that they'll be OK first). Adding stain remover or whitening powders can get white shoes back to their original state.

Avoid the temptation of putting them in the tumble dryer though. Always let the shoes dry naturally at room temperature, padded out with screwed-up newspaper to absorb the moisture. Always store your sneakers away from direct sunlight as this will fade the colour of shoes very easily.

And finally, another simple rule: regular rotation of your wearing routine will mean that all pairs will wear equally instead of just battering one particular model. I guess that means you'll just have to buy more pairs…

254

STORES – LONDON

Foot Patrol
16A St Annes Court
London W1F 0BJ
Tel: +44 (0) 20 7734 6625

Meteor Sports
408–410 Bethnal Green Road
London E2 0DJ
Tel: +44 (0) 20 7739 0707

My Trainers
9 Short Gardens
London WC2H 9AZ
Tel: +44 (0) 20 7379 9700

Offspring
60 Neal Street
London WC2H 9PA
Tel: +44 (0) 20 7497 2463

Size?
33–34 Carnaby Street
London W1F 7DW
Tel: +44 (0) 20 7287 4016

JD Sports
268–269 Oxford Street
London
W1R 1LD
Tel: +44 (0) 20 7491 7677

Sports and Things
213 Streatham High Road
London SW16 6EG
Tel: +44 (0) 20 8677 3810

STORES – USA

Nort 235
235 Eldridge Street
New York NY
Tel: +1 212 777 6102

Alife Rivington Club
158 Rivington Street
New York NY
Tel: +1 212 375 8128

Premium Goods
694 Fulton Street
New York NY
Tel: +1 718 403 9348

Dave's Quality Meat
7 East 3rd Street
New York NY 10003

Prohibit
299 Elizabeth Street
New York NY 10012
Tel: +1 212 219 1469

Zebra Club
1901 1st Seattle
WA 98101

HUF
808 Stutter Street
San Francisco
Tel: +1 415 614 9414

Willy's Workshop
9995 Carmel Mountain Road B10
San Diego, CA 92129
Tel: +1 858 538 5321

STORES – CANADA

GoodFoot
431 Richmond West
Toronto
Tel: +1 416 364 0734

Sportchek
SC Pacific Centre
777 Dunsmuir Street
Vancouver BC V7Y 1A1
Tel: +1 604 687 7668

STORES – AUSTRALIA

Footage
13C Burton Street
Dorlinghurst NSW 2010

STORES – ITALY

Florence
Camping Sport
Via dei Servi 70/72R
Florence

STORES – FRANCE

Zoom Sports
125 Rue St Dennis 75001
Paris

Opium
9 rue du Cygne 75001
Paris
Tel: +33 (0) 1 42 33 55 83

Eight
5 Rue Ste Opportune 75001
Paris
Tel: +33 (0) 1 40 26 87 09

Courir (Les Champs)
104 Avenue des Champs Elysées
75008
Paris
Tel: +33 (0) 1 45 62 50 77

WEBSITES FOR INFORMATION AND SALES

www.altsnk.com
www.atmos-tokyo.com
www.chapterworld.com
www.crookedtongues.com
www.davesqualitymeat.com
www.deadshoescrolls.com
www.eastbay.com
www.ebay.com
www.fatlace.com
www.finishline.com
www.fixins.com
www.footlocker.com
www.footlocker-europe.com
www.foot-patrol.com
www.hufsf.com
www.instyleshoes.com
www.jdsports.co.uk
www.kicksology.net
www.mrsneaker.com
www.niketalk.com
www.officeholdings.co.uk
www.opium-crew.com
www.passover-ss.com
www.retrokid.com
www.sneakerfreaker.com

www.sneakerking.de
www.sneakerpimp.com
www.sneakers.pair.com
www.three3design.com
www.undftd.com
www.vintagekicks.com

BRAND WEBSITES

www.adidas.com
www.asics.com
www.converse.com
www.diadora.com
www.fila.com
www.kswiss.com
www.lacoste.com
www.newbalance.com
www.nike.com
www.pony.com
www.prokeds.com
www.puma.com
www.reebok.com
www.saucony.com
www.vans.com

ACKNOWLEDGMENTS

THANKS TO EVERYBODY WHO HELPED TO MAKE THIS BOOK HAPPEN.

GARY ASPDEN, MIKE CHETCUTI, ANGELA DOLAN, KARMELA AND ALL AT ADIDAS UK. HELEN SWEENEY-DOUGAN, ALISON DAY AND ALL AT PUMA UK. ROBERT WARD AND ALL AT NEW BALANCE UK. JO AT REEBOK UK. FRASER COOKE, DRIEKE LEENKNEGT, KEMI BENJAMAN, AND ALL AT NIKE UK. PETE, KOHEI AND ALL AT FOOT PATROL. RICH, CAT AND CRAIG AT A BATHING APE. JAMES GREENFIELD AND ANTONY BOOTH AT OFFICE UK. ROBERT BROOKES, KEV FREEL, NATHAN ABBOTT, TONY PENFOLD, GRAHAM KERR, LISA PIERCE, MARK BUTLER, SPORTS AND THINGS, MY TRAINERS, SMARTEY, PETE THE BEARD, BEEHIVE STUDIOS CAMDEN, SKATE OF MIND, JOHN AND MARSHALL LAUNDRY, MAXSEM AND JEREMY AT PRIMITIVE, ROY AND DEAN.

INDEX

256